The Future

What Jesus and the Prophets Taught

By

Andrew Ferrier

Dear Reader, This book is to be read with an open Bible. The location of each Scripture is in bold letters. May the Lord bless those who read with faith, hope and love.

Table of Contents

Appendix

How to Interpret Bible Prophecy

Most people are interested in the future. Hot selling tabloid magazines in the checkout lane at the grocery store are filled with predictions of the future, anything from what Hollywood marriage will break-up in the coming year, to when the world is going to end.

Numerous movies and television shows have been made about time travel. Sometimes the character in the movie goes into the future for financial profit. For instance, in the movie, "Back to the Future 2" one of the main characters goes into the future so he can determine the outcome of sporting events. After he returns to his own time he makes millions of dollars betting on the winner of these events.

The expression "hindsight is 20/20" refers to the advantage of knowing the future and is usually spoken after a mistake has been made. If one could know the future, a lot of the heartache in life could be spared. God understands this longing in man to know the future and the Bible, God's book, is filled with literally hundreds of prophecies about the future. In fact, one of the best proofs that the Bible is God's word is the truth of hundreds of fulfilled prophecies. The Bible is the only book in the world that is filled with prophecies that are 100% correct.

The Koran, a holy book to Muslims, does not make even one prediction about the future. The Vedas, the writings of the Hindus, also does not make any predictions about the future. More recently, the writings of Nostradamus have become popular.

While his writings are not religious in nature, he does make quite a number of predictions about the future. Yet, most will agree that at best, Nostradamus was only about 50% correct.

The Bible, on the other hand, is 100% accurate in its predictions about the future. Many of these predictions have already come to pass. But many more remain to be fulfilled in the future, the very near future.

About 25% of the Bible is "prophetic in nature." These predictions could be divided into several categories. There are "near" prophecies. These prophecies were to be fulfilled in the coming months or years. In the book of Jeremiah, chapter 28 verses 15-17, the prophet Jeremiah made a prediction that a false prophet was going to die that year. Sure enough, just two months after Jeremiah made his prediction, the false prophet died.

There are also "far" prophecies that will be fulfilled in the distant future, beyond the lifetime of the prophet. They will be fulfilled hundreds and sometimes thousands of years into the future. There are prophecies about nations, such as Israel, Egypt, Babylon, Syria, and others. The nation of Israel is one of the keys to Bible prophecy.

There are also messianic prophecies about the coming of the Messiah. These can be divided into two categories. Prophecies about the first coming of Jesus, the Messiah, that have been fulfilled and prophecies about his Second Coming.

This book deals primarily with the prophecies about the Second Coming of Jesus Christ. This is referred to in theological terms as "Eschatology," the study of things yet to come. **Revelation 1:3**

God promises a blessing for those who read, hear, and pay attention to prophecy!

The promise for obedience is a promise of a "blessing." The word "blessed" could mean many different things for many different people. God knows you better than you know yourself and will "bless" you in the way of greatest benefit to you when you read and study prophecy! **Revelation 19:10**

Many have come to believe in Jesus through a study of prophecy. A friend of mine told me that he was an atheist before he became a believer in Jesus. "What changed your mind?" I asked him. His answer was "The study of Bible prophecy!" It is my hope and prayer that if you are skeptical about Jesus you will come to faith in Him through reading this book as you see Bible prophecy being fulfilled before your very eyes!

The Rapture and a Jewish Wedding

One of the most anticipated and controversial events yet to happen, is the Rapture of the church. The Rapture is when Jesus returns to "catch up" all who truly believe in Him. The word "rapture" is not found anywhere in the New Testament nor is the word "trinity." Rapture comes from a Latin word meaning to "catch up." (See Latin Vulgate: I Thessalonians 4:17). The church will be "caught up" by Jesus in the "twinkling of an eye" when He will take all true believers in Him to Heaven. There is some disagreement among Christians as to the timing of the Rapture.

There are basically 3 views: The **Pre-tribulation view** states that the Rapture will take place sometime before the start of the seven year Tribulation that ends with the second coming of Christ as described in the book of Revelation.

The **Mid-tribulation view** believes the Rapture will take place sometime in the middle of the seven year Tribulation that ends with the second coming of Christ as described in the book of Revelation.

The **Post-tribulation view** says the Rapture will take place at the second coming of Christ when Jesus returns at the end of the seven year Tribulation. In this view the Rapture and the second coming of Christ are the same event rather than two separate events as in the other two views.

This book will present the evidence for the Pre-Tribulation Rapture. **John 14:1-3** This is the first mention in the Bible of the Rapture of the Church. Jesus is telling His disciples He is going back to his Father's house "to prepare a place for you." It will not only be for them, but for all who believe! He adds that He is going to return, and when he does, He will receive "**you to Myself**." This detail is very important to note, because at the second coming of Christ at the end of the seven year Tribulation, Israel will receive Jesus as their Messiah. (Zechariah 12:10)

Here, at the Rapture, Jesus is receiving Christ followers unto him. [1] The next passage explains that He will then take the Believers back to heaven to that dwelling place He has prepared, just as a groom comes for his bride in a first century Jewish wedding ceremony. **1 Thessalonians 4:13-18**

There is an interesting parallel here between the Rapture of the Church and the first century Jewish custom of marriage. Two thousand years ago the Jewish tradition

---

[1] Showers, Renald, <u>Maranatha: Our Lord Come</u>, p. 155.

of marriage involved a four-step process. In the first step, known as the betrothal, the groom would leave his father's home and travel to the home of his prospective bride where he would negotiate a purchase price with the father of the bride. Once the price was agreed upon, the bride was then officially "set apart" or betrothed, to this groom. They are officially married at this point. The betrothal is not the same as an engagement. An engagement can be broken without going through a divorce, but to break a betrothal, papers of divorce must be submitted. The father of the bride and the groom would drink a glass of wine to show that the marriage contract was legal and binding.

There is a major difference from the Western culture of marriage. The bride and groom would not come together in physical union at this time. The groom at this point would leave his bride and return to his father's home. This begins the second step, the period of separation, which would usually last for around one year. During that year the groom would build a dwelling place for his new bride. The dwelling was usually attached to his father's home. When the dwelling place was finished, the third step was the return of the groom for his bride. As he returned, runners would go ahead of him and shout, "Behold the bride groom comes." He would usually return around midnight or in the wee hours of the morning.

The bride knows the approximate season of the groom's return, but she does not know the exact day or hour. When she hears the shouts of the people running ahead of the groom, she is so excited that she does not wait for her groom to arrive all the way to her home. Instead, she gets up and rushes out to meet him. The groom would then take his bride back to the dwelling place he had prepared for her.

This leads to the fourth step in the wedding, which was the marriage feast. Once at the new dwelling place, a seven day wedding feast would begin. This was when the marriage was finally consummated. [2]

The parallels between Jesus, the Rapture, and the Bride of Christ, the Church, are obvious. Jesus left his father's home and came to this earth to purchase for Himself a bride, which is the Church. The purchase price was His own blood that He shed when He died on the cross for our sin. The Church is now sanctified, or "set-apart," and drinks wine at communion as a symbol to remember that it was the blood of Jesus that paid for sin.

Jesus is now in heaven building a dwelling place for his bride, the Church, as He said to his disciples, "In my father's house are many dwelling places and I go to prepare a place for you."

---

[2] ibid., pp.164-168.

When Jesus returns for His bride He will come at an unexpected day and hour. There will be a great shout of the archangel and a trumpet blast. Then the church, the bride of Jesus, will arise in the twinkling of an eye to meet Jesus in the clouds. He will then take the Church to the dwelling place He has been preparing for almost 2,000 years.

Sometime after the catching up of the bride of Christ, also known as the Rapture, a marriage feast will take place in heaven just as was done in the earthly marriage tradition. It is interesting to note that just as the bride was taken BEFORE the seven day marriage feast, the bride of Christ, the Church, will also be taken BEFORE the seven year Tribulation period spoken of in the book of Revelation.

Copy and paste the code into your web browser for a youtube video on this section: http://www.youtube.com/watch?v=Uh0-VPnndeU

The Rapture and the Feast of Trumpets

God gave seven feasts to the nation of Israel. The feasts were based on an agricultural calendar so that four of the feasts fell in the spring. There was a long break during the summer while the harvest was being brought in. The final three feasts came in the fall to celebrate the ingathering harvest.

Not only were the feasts historical, but they were also prophetic in nature. This means they predicted events coming in the future. For example, the first feast that God gave to Israel, the feast of **Passover**, took place around 1,440 years before Christ. It is recorded in the twelfth chapter of the book of Exodus in the Bible. It was on this feast that God delivered Israel from 400 years of slavery in Egypt. This was the historical aspect of the feast.

At Passover the Jewish people would bring a lamb to the Temple for sacrifice. On this feast day some 1,400 years later, Jesus, the Lamb of God, was sacrificed for sin. Notice that it was on the very day of Passover. As the Priests in the Temple were sacrificing lambs by the thousands, Jesus, the lamb, was being sacrificed on the cross for mankind's sin.

The Apostle Paul makes reference to this in I Corinthians 5:7 where he says, "…For Christ our Passover also has been sacrificed."

Passover was on the first day of a seven day feast known as the feast of **unleavened bread**. During these seven days God commanded Israel to throw out the leaven, which represents sin, and eat only unleavened bread. Today unleavened bread is called, "matzo," and is thin, like a saltine cracker.

The third feast God gave to Israel was called the "**feast of first-fruits**." It was during the same week as the feast of unleavened bread and it was always on the "day after the Sabbath." The Sabbath is Saturday, therefore, the celebration of the feast of first-fruits would be on Sunday.

On this feast the High Priest would make a special sacrifice and perform a wave offering. Not only did Jesus die on Passover, a Jewish feast day, but He also arose from the dead on a Jewish feast day—the feast of first fruits! The Apostle Paul makes reference to this in 1 Corinthians 15:20 where he says, "But now Christ has been raised from the dead, the **first fruits** of those who are asleep."

After the feast of first-fruits, the Priests in the Temple would count seven weeks, plus one day, to the next feast known in Hebrew as "Shavuot" or the "**feast of**

weeks." It is better known by its Greek name, **Pentecost.**

What happened on the feast of Pentecost? Acts, chapter 2, tells us the Spirit of God came down from Heaven and filled the believers and this marked the start of the Church.

The first four of the Jewish feasts have been fulfilled, but three more remain to be fulfilled. This is now the church age, a time to be bringing in a harvest of souls, just as the harvest would be brought in during the summertime in Israel. Jesus said, "The harvest is great but the workers are few." (Matthew 9:37, 38)

The next three feasts to be fulfilled are the fall feasts of Israel. They come in **September/October** but never on the same day. The dates change from year to year because the feasts are on the Jewish calendar, which is a lunar calendar while the current calendar is a solar calendar.

The next feast on the Jewish calendar yet to be fulfilled is the **feast of trumpets.** Prophetically, this feast speaks of the Rapture of the church. As the Apostle Paul referred to Passover and First-fruits in the book of 1 Corinthians, he also makes a reference to the feast of trumpets in 1 **Corinthians 15:51, 52.**

Paul is describing the Rapture of the church. He says it will take place "at the last trumpet." What is meant by the last trumpet?

On the feast of trumpets, there are 100 trumpet blasts sounded in the synagogue. There are four different types of trumpet blasts. They are:

Tekiah—one long blast.

Shevarim—3 short calls.

Teruah—9 short calls.

Tekiah Gedolah—the great or LAST trumpet.

The "Tekiah Gedolah" is the very last trumpet call sounded on the feast of trumpets. It is to be blown and held out as long as the trumpet player can possibly hold it.

When Paul says the Rapture will happen at the last trumpet, it is very likely he is talking about the last trumpet of the feast of trumpets. After all, he has already talked about two other Jewish feasts in the book of 1Corinthians.

The first set of Jewish feasts were fulfilled by Jesus Christ exactly on the day of their feasts. Does this mean the Rapture of the church will happen on the day of the feast of trumpets? Only time will tell.

The feast after the feast of Trumpets really is not a feast at all. It is a fast day known in Hebrew as "Yom Kippur," the Day of Atonement. It is the most solemn day in the Jewish year, for it was on this day the High Priest of Israel would enter the Holy of Holies in the Temple to make atonement for the sins of the nation of Israel.

The High Priest could enter the Holy of Holies only one day a year—Yom Kippur. Only the High Priest was allowed to enter the Holy of Holies. When he entered he had to have blood from a prescribed, sacrificed animal to sprinkle on the mercy seat of the ark. If these strict rules were not followed, God Himself would strike him dead. (Leviticus 16)

Yom Kippur prophetically speaks of the seven year Tribulation, which will follow the Rapture of the church. The fact that this feast follows the feast of trumpets is also an argument for the Rapture happening before the seven year Tribulation.

Just as Yom Kippur was to be a day of suffering as God told Israel to "humble your souls" (Leviticus 16:31), so the seven year Tribulation will be a time of affliction and humbling not only for Israel but for the whole world.

Five days after Yom Kippur, the final feast God gave to Israel, the Feast of Tabernacles, is celebrated. Prophetically, this feast speaks of the time Jesus will return to earth after the seven year Tribulation and set up his kingdom on this earth for 1,000 years. During this time God will dwell or "Tabernacle" among men. [3]

What a beautiful picture God has laid out for us in these seven feasts He gave to the Nation of Israel. How exciting to know,

---

[3] Zola Levitt, Levitt Letter, Vol. 20 #9.

they are not just festivals that happened hundreds and even thousands of years ago. They speak of things to come in the days ahead! Copy and paste the code into your web browser for a youtube video on this section: http://www.youtube.com/watch?v=sVQr-a8nJtI

   1 Thessalonians 5:2-9 contains a clue to the timing of the Rapture. The phrase, "Day of the Lord" is a reference to the seven year Tribulation spoken of in the book of Revelation. Here the Apostle Paul says this seven-year hell on earth will start suddenly and will catch people by surprise, much like a women goes into labor unexpectedly. He goes on to say the "day of the Lord" or seven year Tribulation will NOT overtake believers in Jesus. In other words, believers in Jesus will not have to go through this terrible time! He concludes by saying "God has not destined us for wrath." The word "wrath" is another reference to the seven year Tribulation which believers are not destined to experience.
   Another relevant Scripture is **Revelation 3:10**. In his message to the church Jesus says He will keep the church from the "hour of testing," which is another name for the seven year Tribulation. The Greek word for "from" has the idea of "out of." So Jesus will keep the church "out of"

the seven year Tribulation.

Indeed, in Revelation chapters 1-3 the church is referred to over twenty different times. However, in chapters 6-19, which deal with the seven years of the Tribulation, the word "church" is not found even once.

In fact, John begins to use the word "saints" for those who become believers during the Tribulation. While believers in Jesus today are saints, so also were people in the Old Testament. The fact that the church is not found in Revelation 6-19 is an argument from silence, but is a powerful one and puts the burden of proof on those who say the church is going through the Tribulation.

The Great Alien Deception

The Scripture indicates that the end times will be a time of deception. Jesus said in Matthew 24:11, **"And many false prophets shall rise, and shall deceive many."** The Apostle Paul also wrote of a coming "great delusion" or "deception" in **2 Thessalonians 2:11.**

One of the greatest deceptions of our day is being played out before our very eyes almost on a daily basis, and yet most are completely unaware it is even going on. It is on television programming almost nightly. It has been the topic of numerous documentaries. It permeates the film and movie making industry. And it is the topic of an ever-increasing number of books and magazines.

The topic is UFO's (unidentified foreign objects), aliens from outer space. They have captured the attention and imagination of our world today. How many main stream movies and TV shows have been about aliens or involved meeting aliens on other planets?

Take for example, "**The War of the Worlds,**" which was a fictional radio show about an alien space ship landing on earth. It was broadcast in 1938 from New York City the night before Halloween as though it were a real live news event. It is estimated that of the some six million people who heard the CBS broadcast; 1.7 million believed it to be true, and 1.2 million were genuinely frightened. Some even took to the streets to evacuate a city that was about to be "invaded by aliens." [4]

Other popular shows include: Star Trek, Star Wars, Close Encounters of the Third Kind, The X-Files, E.T., First Contact, Lost in Space, Unsolved Mysteries, Independence Day, Men in Black I, Men in Black II, Aliens I, Aliens II, Aliens III, Alien vs. Predator I, Alien vs. Predator II, not to mention the countless cartoon programs for kids featuring aliens. Even the Indiana Jones movie was about aliens. It is all part of the great end times deception.

Of interest is the fact that Israel is recognized as a UFO world **hot spot**, with an unsurpassed quantity and quality of evidence. Numerous UFO sightings have been reported by thousands of people in Israel. So much so that the Israeli Knesset

---

4

http://en.wikipedia.org/wiki/The_War_of_th e _Worlds_%28radio%29 even discussed the phenomenon on February 12, 1997 with no resolution. [5] Researchers note that the sightings in that part of the world appear to be occurring almost exclusively over Israel rather than over other countries in the Middle East.

Before we go any further, first a little background. **Matthew 24:37** What was it like in the days of Noah? **Genesis 6:1-4** In every instance in the Old Testament where the phrase, **"Sons of God"** is used, it is always a reference to angels. Even the Septuagint (LXX), the Greek translation of the Old Testament written around 200 B.C. translated this phrase **"angels."** [6]

For 120 years before the flood Satan attempted to stop the coming of the Messiah by having some of his fallen angels enter into sexual relations with earthly women. The result of this union was an offspring of giants apparently with super human strength.

In response to this, God sent a flood that destroyed the world including the perverted offspring of these fallen angels. The Apostle Peter seems to confirm this in 2 Peter 2:4 where he makes reference to **"the angels that sinned"** in the "days of Noah."

Now, run forward in time to Planet

---

[5] Chuck Missler, Alien Encounters: The Secret Behind the UFO Phenomenon.
[6] Arnold Fruchtenbaum, The Book of Genesis, p. 145-146.

22

Earth and the 21st century A.D. Is the same thing happening all over again? Strangely enough it is! But this is to be expected based on the fact that Jesus said the end times would be, **"As it was in the days of Noah."**

About 2% of the population in America claims to have seen an alien spaceship and literally millions of people around the world claim to have been abducted by aliens. The sheer volume of unrelated eye witnesses around the world should tell us something is going on.

In 1997, a movie came out called "Fire in the Sky" which was the true story of a man who **claimed** to have been abducted by aliens and taken to their spaceship where they performed medical experiments on him. This was not an isolated event as millions now claim to have had some contact with aliens. Amazingly, some women who have been abducted by aliens report to having had a sexual relation or undergoing medical experiments on the sexual part of their body by aliens. Some men have reported a similar experience. There is a man in Canada by the name of Claude Vorilhon who claims to be the offspring of a union between an alien and a human woman. [7]

Claude was born in September, 1946. He says aliens contacted him at the

---

[7]

http://en.widipedia.org/wiki/Ra%C3%ABlis m

age of 28 as he was hiking near his home in France on a foggy day. He saw the blinking red light of an aircraft on the ground. As he approached the craft he says he noticed a small child-sized occupant. The being was smiling, and had a glow around his body. He had a **Star of David** on his space suit with a **swastika** in the middle of it. This creature spoke to him in French and claimed the ability to speak all of Earth's languages. Claude says he met with these aliens on six different occasions during which they gave him a commentary on key portions of the Bible. Of interest is their claim that the Bible is mistakenly interpreted and they are the real "Elohim," the gods who created us. They changed Claude's name to "Rael" meaning "light worker."

Claude, who now goes by the name "Rael" is spreading the word that aliens are getting ready to reveal themselves to our planet. To prepare for their visit he claims they want him to build a welcome center in a neutral location. This welcome center would be the fulfillment of the rebuilding of the Temple as prophesied in the Bible.

But this is not the half of it. If these reports are true, these beings are actually fallen angels of Satan **masquerading** as aliens. They have quite a bit to say about the "coming evacuation from earth."

The alien phenomenon we are witnessing today has permeated our culture and is, in fact, **demons masquerading as aliens**. Listen to the message these aliens, who are really demons, are telling people. Where is their message being given? These demons, or aliens, have written **whole books**. These are offered for sale at Borders book store, or Barnes and Noble, or Amazon.com. How does an alien or demon write a book you ask?

The aliens, or demons, communicate in one of 4 different ways.

Channeling: In this method a human host puts him or herself into a trance and allows the alien to speak, very similar to what is done in a séance when people try to communicate with the dead. The human host then writes what he or she has heard.

Auto-writing. To do this the supposed alien takes over the motor skills of the writing hand of the host human and begins writing a book or letter to communicate.

A third method is called, **"step-in."** In this the alien (or really demon) steps into the body of the host human and takes control of the host's body which is really demon possession.

A fourth way they communicate is through **abduction**. Aliens forcibly take someone away to their "spaceship." They quite often give them a message. [8]

---

[8] Chuck Missler, <u>Alien Encounters: The Secret Behind the UFO Phenomenon</u>.

What are these demons telling people? Every part of their message is in direct contradiction to the Word of God. This is indeed the "doctrine of demons" the Apostle Paul spoke of in the End Times in **1 Timothy 4:1.**

Of interest is the fact that the message of the aliens is of a philosophical and religious nature, rather than scientific and technological. If they are really here to help us solve our environmental problems and evolve to the next level as they say, why not share some technological information to help us solve our energy crisis, cure cancer, or at least get a faster internet connection? But no, they seem fixated on a new age ecumenical religious message. As **John Ankerberg** and **John Weldon** ask in their book, **"The Facts on UFOs"**: "…how credible is it to think that thousands of extraterrestrials would fly millions or billions of light years simply to teach New Age philosophy, deny Christianity, and support the occult?" [2]

Here are some of the things they are teaching: They are telling people that God did not create life on this planet as recorded in Genesis chapter one, but rather they, the aliens, seeded this planet with microscopic life and that we have evolved over millions of years.[10]

[9] John Ankerberg, <u>Facts on UFO'S.</u>
[10] Chuck Missler, <u>Alien Encounters: The</u>

Interestingly, some scientists who believe in evolution are coming to believe this same thing as they realize that life is too complex to have evolved by pure chance. In Ben Stein's recent movie, "Expelled: No Intelligence Allowed," Richard Dawkins, considered one of the world's leading evolutionists says: "It could be that at some earlier time somewhere in the universe a civilization evolved by, probably, some kind of Darwinian means to a very, very high level of technology and designed a form of life that they seeded onto, perhaps, this planet. Now that is a possibility, and an intriguing possibility." [11]

Others teach that we can evolve into gods like them. Does that sound familiar? That is the same lie that Satan told Eve in the Garden of Eden. **Genesis 3:5**

Many promote a "Mother Earth" concept and the idea that the earth should be worshiped, a belief common in pantheism, witchcraft, and the New Age Movement. [12] It is similar to what is being taught by the "Global Warming" theorists. The warning is that if we don't stop polluting "mother earth," apocalyptic type problems will begin to plague our planet. Earthquakes, floods,

---

Secret Behind the UFO Phenomenon.
[11] Ben Stein, Expelled: No Intelligence Allowed, 2008
[12] Chuck Missler, Alien Encounters: The Secret Behind the UFO Phenomenon

typhoons and hurricanes will be commonplace. These will be used to explain away the judgments of the Tribulation period. As God is pouring out His judgments on earth because of man's sin, many will refuse to acknowledge God's hand in it, but will instead point to "global warming" and blame all of the acts of God on pollution and an enlarged "carbon footprint." **Revelation 16:8, 9**

It is as if a bank robber is excused from stealing thousands of dollars from a bank, but is then thrown in prison for not recycling a plastic bottle. The aliens are teaching that man stands at the threshold of a quantum leap of evolution that will abolish religious and governmental systems as we know them. It will bring the "universal brotherhood of man." They say that we humans must form a One World Government and unite into a One World Religion or we are doomed. [13]

The Bible prophesied the setting up of a one world government in the end times in **Daniel 7:23, 24** that will be run by the anti-Christ.

The aliens teach that Jesus, Moses, Buddha, Mohammed, and Krishna are all ascended masters of light, who were appointed to be bearers of truth in different generations. Thus, no one religion is any more correct than any other and truth is

---

[13] ibid.

defined by the individual. There is no absolute truth. [14]

This is definitely the opposite of what Jesus said in **John 14:6.**

There also seems to be a fascination with Jesus. They teach that Jesus was actually half man and half alien. He was a wise and holy man, the most ever to walk our planet. However, a frequent message from the aliens is that Jesus was not God. The aliens say Jesus ascended to heaven on an alien space ship, but very soon he is going to come again via space ship. [15] (Could this actually be a reference to the coming of the anti-Christ?)

Intriguingly, the aliens have quite a bit to say about the **Rapture of the church.** They don't call it the Rapture. They call it a "mass evacuation." They are saying that Earth's population needs to be decreased to move to the next level of evolution. There are millions of people who are "out of vibration" with Mother Earth and need to be removed from her to bring in the coming new age. A coming cleansing is about to take place they say. In fact, even at this very hour they claim there are space ships surrounding earth ready to take these people away. If man does not change his ways, then Mother Earth, who is reaching for a higher frequency, will bring about a cleansing

---

[14] ibid.
[15] ibid.

which will balance it once again. The people who will be taken from the planet do not belong here. They do not fit here. They are stopping the harmony of Mother Earth. They have thought patterns of the past that are holding Mother Earth back. [16]

You can guess who they might be talking about. Yes, Christians. When the time comes millions of people will leave the planet at the same time. This mass evacuation will happen very suddenly, even "in the twinkling of an eye!" (Amazingly, they use the same wording as Scripture.) Aliens explain that their smaller spacecraft will lift millions of people simultaneously and then transport them to larger ships, deeper in space, where there is room for millions of people.

Quote: "Our rescue ships will be able to come in close enough in the twinkling of an eye to set the lifting beams in operation in a moment. And all over the globe where events warrant it, this will be the method of evacuation. Mankind will be lifted, levitated shall we say, by the beams from our smaller ships. These smaller craft will in turn taxi the persons to the larger ships overhead, higher in the atmosphere, where there is ample space and quarters and supplies for millions of people." A message from ET of the Ashtar Command Project World Evacuation, 1993.

---

[16] ibid.

They are getting ready to explain away the Rapture when it happens. Notice that Satan and his demons are trying to explain away the Pre-Tribulation rapture of the church, and not a Post-Tribulation rapture! This is an additional reason for the preaching and teaching the Pre-Tribulation Rapture of the church.

When the Rapture happens, people who have heard the teaching of the Pre-Tribulation Rapture possibly may not be deceived into thinking that it was aliens who have taken millions of people from the earth. They will understand it was the Rapture of the church by Jesus Himself. This will give them the incentive to repent and be saved. Christians who argue against the Pre-Tribulation rapture unwittingly are aiding and abetting the enemy's great deception.

The aliens say that very soon earthly governments, with our assistance, will reveal to the world a truth they have been hiding. It is the fact that they have been interacting with extra-terrestrials for many years.

The public is now ready for the truth. The conditioning by TV, radio, books, and magazines has done its job. It is now safe to reveal that we are here!

And one more message from the aliens: "Far from evil sorcerers of Satan, we are in reality, messengers of light. [17] 2

---

[17] ibid.

Corinthians 11:14
It is our job as believers to expose these falsehoods and get the word out. Jesus is coming soon. Tell your unsaved friends, "Hey, if I suddenly vanish along with millions of other believers in Jesus, it is not the aliens who have taken us. The rapture of the church has just taken place, and you have been **left behind**. But you can still be saved through simple faith in the death, burial, and resurrection of Jesus!"

Copy and paste the code to your web browser for a you tube video on this section:
http://www.youtube.com/watch?v=7NGF8ih Wa9Y

Just Before the Clock Strikes Twelve

The Rapture of the church is "imminent." This means it could happen at any time. It could happen today, tomorrow, next week, etc. The start of the Tribulation period, however, is not imminent. There are certain things that must happen before the Tribulation period can start. This is necessary to allow for the Rapture to be imminent.

The Tribulation period will start when the anti-Christ comes on the scene and signs a covenant with Israel. We learn this from **Daniel 9:27**. Once this covenant is signed, the Tribulation period is set in motion.

These are the seven events that have, or will, happen before the start of the Tribulation period.

#1 World Wars

The disciples of Jesus asked him three questions in **Matthew 24:1-3**.

First, "When will these things be?" In other words, when will the destruction of the Temple take place? The answer to this question is not given here in Matthew, but is answered in **Luke 21:20-24**. The Jewish Temple in Jerusalem was destroyed in a war between the Jews and the Romans in 70 A.D. in a direct fulfillment of the prophecy of Jesus.

Second, "What will be the sign of your coming?" In **Matthew 24:4-31**, Jesus answers their second question. In verse 30 he says that His coming will be seen clearly by the whole world.

The "sign of his coming" is the visible, personal return of Jesus back to earth in power and great glory.

The third question the disciples asked Jesus, "What will be the sign of the end of the age?" This is answered in **Matthew 24:4-7**. Here, Jesus says there would be false Messiahs who would deceive many. Over the years there have been many false Messiahs. Recent false Messiahs include David Koresh of the Branch Davidians [18] and Jim Jones of the People's Temple who led his followers on a suicide mission in Guyana. [19]

A more recent Jewish false Messiah was Rabbi Menachem Schneerson, a Lubavitch Rabbi who was born in Russia, but made his home in Brooklyn, N.Y.[20] It

---

18

http://en.wikipedia.org/wiki/David_Koresh.
[19] http://en.wikipedia.org/wiki/Jim_Jones.
20

was during the Gulf War, in 1991, when America went into Kuwait to kick Iraq out, that Rabbi Schneerson made some predictions that seemed to have come true. He was at this time, hailed as the Messiah. He didn't claim to be the Messiah, but he also didn't deny it. He had about 30,000 followers, many of whom claim to have witnessed miracles performed by him. He was an elderly man, in his 90's, at the time he was hailed as the Messiah.

A few years after that, Rabbi Schneerson died. But, on the third day, many of his followers gathered at his grave hoping he would rise from the dead. (Sound familiar? Jesus arose from the dead on the third day!) However, this Rabbi did not. He has many dedicated followers who still believe he could be the Messiah.

Many false Messiahs have come over the years. Jesus predicted this. He also said there would be wars and rumors of wars. Over the last 2,000 years there have been many wars and very few years of peace. In verse six Jesus says these signs of wars, and false Messiahs are **not** a sign of his coming. First he answered their question in the negative. Then in **Matthew 24:7** Jesus begins to answer their question in the positive.

The expression, "Nation against

---

nation, kingdom against kingdom," is a Jewish idiom for World War. [21] Jesus is saying that when you see world-wide war, it is a sign that you are now living in the last days. This has been the first generation to see world war. World War I was hoped to be the "war to end all wars." Shortly after that, World War II came along. Now it is not "if", but "when" will be the start of World War III.

Jesus went on to say there would be famines. In the 1900's on average, one million people a year died from starvation and related illness. Scientists tell us we are only one bad harvest away from tens of millions of people starving to death. [22]

Jesus also said there would be pestilence. Aids, Ebola, bird flu, swine flu, and many other killer diseases have the capability to kill millions of people. This could also be a reference to germ warfare. Just recently, Swine flu has begun to worry scientists. In the early 1900's a similar flu, the Spanish flu, had a mortality rate of only 2%, and yet it went on to kill some 50 million people. [23]

Finally, Jesus spoke of earthquakes.

---

[21] Arnold Fructenbaum, <u>Footsteps of the Messiah,</u> p.634.

[22] http://en.wikipedia.org/wiki/List_of_famines #20th_century.

[23] http://en.wikipedia.org/wiki/Spanish_flu.

On December 26, 2004, a 9.0 quake triggered a tsunami that killed approximately a quarter of a million people in Indonesia and India. [24] This was the fourth most powerful quake ever measured, and another sign we are living in the last days.

#2 The Rebirth of the State of Israel

A second thing we would expect before the start of the Tribulation period is the rebirth of the State of Israel. According to **Daniel 9:27**, the Tribulation period will start when the anti-Christ signs a covenant with Israel. In order for the anti-Christ to sign a covenant with Israel, there has to be a State of Israel. In May of 1948, Israel proclaimed her independence, and for the first time in almost 2,000 years the State of Israel was reborn.

The story of the rebirth of Israel is an amazing one in itself. It all started rather quietly in the country of France in the late 1890's. A Jewish captain in the French army by the name of Alfred Dreyfus was accused and convicted of treason. Because he was Jewish there were anti-Semitic attacks against the Jewish community in France where, up until that time, he had lived in peace and quiet. Later it was discovered that Mr. Dreyfus was actually innocent, but the

---

24

http://en.wikipedia.org/wiki/2004_Indian_O cean_earthquake.

damage had already been done. [25]

Another Jewish man by the name of Theodore Herzl saw how quickly anti-Semitism could rear its ugly head. He therefore proposed a homeland for his people, a place where they could live in safety without fear of persecution. At first Herzl considered Africa or America as a homeland for his people, but he eventually came to the conclusion that the only place for his people was back in their Biblical homeland of Israel.

Herzl wrote a book entitled, "The Jewish State," and in 1891 held the first Zionist congress in Basil, Switzerland. He predicted that within fifty years the modern State of Israel would be reborn. He was off by just a few months. [26] Known as the father of modern Zionism, Herzl's dream set the gears in motion for the return of the Jewish people in mass back to their homeland. There has always been a Jewish presence in the land of Israel, but now more Jews were beginning to trickle back. This trickle would turn into a flood of Jewish refuges during WWII.

It was actually WWI that prepared the land for the return of its God-given

---

25

http://en.wikipedia.org/wiki/Dreyfus_affair.
26

http://en.wikipedia.org/wiki/Theodore_Herzl
.

38

owners. In WWI the British had captured this sliver of land from the Turks. It was also during this war that a Jewish scientist by the name of Chaim Wiseman, who would later become the first Prime Minister of Israel, invented an explosive that helped the British win the war. After the war, as a show of gratitude, the Queen wrote Wiseman a blank check and said, "What would you like?"

He answered, "The establishment of a homeland for my people in Palestine" (as the piece of land was called at that time.) Her majesty's government drew up a declaration called, "The Balfour Declaration." It said,

"Her Majesty's government views with favour the establishment in Palestine of a national home for the Jewish people, and will use their best endeavors to facilitate the achievement of this object, it being clearly understood that nothing shall be done which may prejudice the civil and religious rights of existing non-Jewish communities in Palestine, or the rights and political status enjoyed by Jews in any other country."[27]

The door was now open for Jewish people to begin returning to the land of Israel. There was only one problem. No one

---

[27]

http://en.wikipedia.org/wiki/Balfour_Declar ation_of_1917.

wanted to live in a malaria-infested, swamp land. The Jewish people at that time were quite at home in Europe with the bulk of them (some 3 million) living in Warsaw, Poland. That is, until WWII came along. WWI provided the land for the people--and WWII prepared the people for the land. In WWII Adolf Hitler rose to power and began to systematically exterminate the Jewish people. Thousands fled from Hitler and his henchmen. For many of them the only place of escape was to the land of Israel.

After WWII, the British still maintained control of "Palestine," as it was then called. By the way, the name "Palestine" is a derogatory name coined by the Romans for the land of Israel after the Jewish revolt around 136 A.D. After the Romans put down this revolt they renamed the land "Palestine" after the ancient enemies of Israel, the Philistines. It was an effort to erase any Jewish identity to the land. [28]

Now there was so much armed conflict going on between the Jews and the Arabs that the British finally decided to pull out of the land and let those two groups fight it out. Israel saw this as her opportunity to have a homeland. After the last British soldier had left, in May of 1948, she proclaimed her independence. There was

---

[28] http://en.wikipedia.org/wiki/Palestine.

rejoicing in the streets of Tel-Aviv and in Jewish communities around the world as, for the first time in over 2,000 years, the Jews controlled the land. The rejoicing, however, was short lived, as the next day the tiny, new country was invaded by several of the surrounding Arab nations, purposing to "drive the Jews into the Mediterranean."

In 1948, the tiny, new Jewish state, out-manned and out-gunned, with no tanks or air force, managed to win the first of several wars forced upon it. Some believe God miraculously intervened. Today, close to five million Jewish people from over one hundred different countries call the land of Israel their home. Some ten million Jews still live outside the land known as the Diaspora. Over 2,500 years ago the Scripture foretold they would return.

At the urging of the invading Arabs, tens of thousands of Palestinian Arabs left their property in the tiny land, fearing they too would be swept up in the fighting. The Jews urged them to stay and fight alongside them. Those Palestinians who stayed, still live in the land of Israel today. Those who left would be used as political pawns, to blame Israel for the whole Palestinian problem.

Jordan, Kuwait, and other Moslem countries have expelled literally thousands of Palestinians from their lands, but nothing is said of it. [29] Yet the Palestinians, who left Israel on their own accord, are brought up over and over again as an example of "atrocities by Israel."

While it is not the purpose of this book to deal with this controversial issue, Israel has not been without fault in her treatment of the Palestinians, but, for the most part she has acted with fairness and compassion. Israel has built schools, hospitals, and more for the Palestinians. Palestinians are included in the functioning of the government all the way up to the Knesset. At times they have even sat on the Israeli cabinet. [30]

Newscasts choose to give the impression that all Palestinians are living in poverty because of Israel, rather than the fact that the Palestinian leadership, including the late Yasser Arafat, continues to embezzle billions of dollars directed to relief for the west bank residents, while the people living in the Gaza Strip sit in abject poverty.

The amazing miracle of the Jews regaining the land which God promised to them, an event which defied all odds, has not been understood by all Christians as a fulfillment of Biblical prophecy. Instead, two views have arisen today concerning the State of Israel.

---

[29] http://www.factsandlogic.org/ad_28.html.
[30] Stand With Us, Israel 101, p. 40.

First View

One Christian view of Israel, and probably the main view of most Christians today, is that the rebirth of Israel is of **no** prophetic significance and is **not** a fulfillment of Biblical prophecy. This belief is commonly held today by those who are taught Covenant Theology, or Replacement Theology. Their belief is that God is finished with Israel and therefore, the Church has taken Israel's place. To them, the rebirth of Israel is a theological embarrassment and they are not quite sure what to do with it. [31] This will be discussed in the chapter entitled, Covenant Theology Confusion.

Second View

Another Christian view of the rebirth of Israel is that the return of the Jews back to their homeland, even though in unbelief, is a fulfillment of Bible prophecy. It is based on the fact that the Scriptures speak of a return of the Jews back to their homeland, first in unbelief, and then in belief in Jesus, as Messiah. **Ezekiel 20:34-38** Notice in this passage that **first** there is the re-gathering and **then** the rebels are purged out of Israel, indicating that first the return is in unbelief,

---

[31] Arnold Fructenbaum, The Modern State of Israel in Bible Prophecy, p. 3.

with belief coming later.

Ezekiel 36:24-27 is a very clear passage showing the re-gathering of Israel is first in unbelief, with belief in Jesus as the Messiah to follow: Some might ask, "Could not the Jews be driven from their homeland and wander around for a couple of hundred years and then return? Who knows, maybe they could be driven out again and again, 3 or 4 or 5 times? How can we know that this return of the Jews is "the" return spoken of in Scripture?" The answer to this can be found in Isaiah chapter 11. Here Isaiah writes that there will only be **two** end time returns of the Jews back to their homeland.

Isaiah 11:11

As seen in the previous Scriptures, the first return will be in unbelief. To this date almost 5 million Jews have returned back to the land of Israel, with very few being Christians. At the mid-point of the Tribulation period, the antichrist will begin to persecute the Jews and many of them will flee from the land of Israel. This is what Jesus spoke of in **Matthew 24:16**.

They will then be re-gathered at the end of the Tribulation period according to **Matthew 24:31**. This will be the second and final re-gathering of the Jewish people back to their homeland. This time they gather in belief that Jesus is the Messiah. Since the Scriptures speak of only two returns and the first has already occurred, there will not be a third or fourth return. The return in unbelief is a yet to be fulfilled Bible prophecy. [32]

#3 A One World Government

A fifth thing that should happen before the start of the Tribulation is the establishment of a one World government. This is according to **Daniel 7:23, 24**.

This final kingdom will conquer the whole earth. Some think today that the European Union (EU) is this kingdom, but the EU includes only a few nations on earth. This final one-world government will include not only the European nations but every nation on the face of the earth. At some point after the one world government has been created, it will then be broken down into ten kingdoms that will be governed by ten kings. That leads to the sixth event.

#4 The Rise of the Anti-Christ

At some point after the One World Government has been set up and then divided into ten kingdoms, the antichrist will rise to power according to **Daniel 7:24**. He will subdue three of the ten kings, giving him more control and power than all the rest of them. A more detailed description of the antichrist will be discussed when

---

[32] ibid. p. 102,103.

Revelation, chapter 6 is examined.

#5 An Interval of False Peace and Safety

The seventh and final event that should happen before the start of the Tribulation period is a time of peace and safety. The seven year Tribulation period will be the most horrific time the world has ever seen or ever will see. Yet, almost ironically, it will start out rather peacefully. This is a calm before the storm according to **1 Thessalonians 5: 1-3.**

The phrase, "day of the Lord" is a reference here to the whole seven years of the Tribulation period. Paul says the Tribulation will start unexpectedly, as a "thief in the night." It will start at a time when people believe that "peace and safety" have finally been achieved in the world.

Remember, the Tribulation period starts when the antichrist makes a covenant or treaty of peace with Israel. According to **Daniel 9:27**, "he" (the antichrist), will confirm the covenant with many (Israel) for one week (seven years). This will quickly turn out to be the most devastating time in the history of the world.

#6 Close to Construction: Rebuilding of the Temple in Jerusalem

A third thing expected prior to the

start of the Tribulation period is the rebuilding of the Temple in Jerusalem. Several passages of Scripture bring this out. **Daniel 9:27**

According to this passage, "he," the antichrist, will enter the Temple and desecrate it. This will happen at the mid-point of the seven year Tribulation period. Jesus also spoke of this in **Matthew 24:15.**

Another passage which speaks of the anti-Christ desecrating the Temple is in **2 Thessalonians 2:1-4**. This passage also tells us something about the timing of the Rapture:

Verse one is talking about the Rapture. When the Apostle Paul says "brethren," he is talking to believers. When he talks about "**our** gathering unto him (Christ)" he is referring to Christians being gathered to Jesus. This happens at the Rapture. Paul also taught this doctrine in his first letter to the Thessalonians in chapter 4 which has already been discussed.

In verse two, someone apparently had circulated a letter or rumor that the "Day of the Lord" had already started. The "Day of the Lord" is another name for the seven year Tribulation period. The Christians were experiencing persecution and were thinking this was the Tribulation. But, Paul says, "No, wait a minute, you're not in the tribulation period yet."

Two things must happen before the

tribulation can start. Paul writes that there will be the "falling away first." This comes from the Greek word, "apostacya" from which we get the English word, "apostasy." This could be talking about apostasy in the church, or a general apostasy of evil in the world. Either way, we are certainly living in a time of apostasy. Even in the days of the Apostle Paul, apostasy was beginning to creep into the church.

The second thing Paul says will happen is the revealing of "the man of sin" or the antichrist. He is also called the "son of perdition." In fact, there are ten different names given for the antichrist in Scripture. [33] Paul says the antichrist will come on the scene after the Rapture of the church but before the start of the Tribulation. Remember, in verse one, Paul says that believers in Jesus will be gathered to Jesus. That is the Rapture. Then there will be apostasy and the revealing of the antichrist which will bring on the "Day of the Lord" or the start of the Tribulation period. This passage is clearly showing us that the Rapture will happen prior to the start of the Tribulation period. Then in verse 4, Paul says the antichrist will enter the Temple and set himself up as God. This will happen at the mid-point of the Tribulation. For the antichrist to set himself up in the Temple, there has to be a temple! Right now there is

___

[33] ibid. p.207.

no Jewish temple on the Temple Mount in Jerusalem. But, the Temple will be rebuilt, either prior to the start of the Tribulation or even during the first half of the Tribulation according to these passages.

The Movement in Israel to Rebuild the Temple

In 1988 a group was started in Israel that was called, The Temple Institute. They are making preparations for the rebuilding of the Temple. They have already made the clothing to be worn by the High Priests and the other priests who will minister in the Temple. They have remade the dishes for use in the Temple. The dishes are made of solid gold and silver. Literally hundreds of different vessels are ready for use in the rebuilt Temple.

They have constructed the table of showbread, the altar of incense, and the golden menorah, over-laid with pure gold at a cost of millions of dollars. The half ton menorah is on display in Jerusalem.

There are now schools in Israel training Jewish men to be priests and teaching them how to minister in the Temple, and once again to make sacrifices.[34]

They have also been involved in the search for the "red heifer." In 2003, a red heifer was born on a kibbutz in Israel. When

---

[34] http://www.thetempleinstitute.com

it was born, the Orthodox Jews in Israel became very excited and went to see it. They said this was a sign the Messiah was coming soon. [35] The ashes of the red heifer will be needed to begin the sacrifices in the Temple according to Numbers 19. Jewish law says a red heifer can have no more than two white hairs on it to be considered red. Until 2003 one did not exist in Israel.

The ashes of the heifer will be used for the cleansing of the priests. The ashes are placed on the priest's right ear, right thumb, and right toe for purification.

Numbers 19

There is now a worldwide search for Jewish men from the family of "Cohen." It is very interesting that in the days of Jesus, every Jewish person knew which tribe he was from. Today, all of the tribes have lost their identity except for the tribe of Levi. Jewish people with the last name of "Levi, Levinson, Levy" or some variation of this name, are descended from the tribe of Levi. Jewish people with the last name of "Cohen," are from the priestly family within the tribe of Levi. Israel is searching for men with this last name who would be willing to live in Jerusalem and minister as priests in the Temple.

Another group in Israel is called, "The Temple Mount Faithful." They have a cornerstone ready to be placed in the

---

[35] http://www.templemountfaithful.org

foundation of the third Temple. They have made a model of the third Temple and the plans for constructing it are ready.

The only thing holding back the building of the Temple is the Dome of the Rock. This golden dome is the third most holy site to Islam and sits atop the Temple Mount in Jerusalem. Some feel the dome sits on the exact location of the Jewish Temple and therefore would need to be moved before the Jewish Temple could be built. Others believe the Jewish Temple actually stood to the north of the Dome of the Rock and could be rebuilt next to it without moving the Dome.

Some Moslems would like to build a minaret on the Temple Mount to give them greater claim to the Mount. The Moslem call to prayer is broadcast from the minaret to the surrounding community over loud speakers five times a day, including 3 A.M.!

The Scripture is clear, however, that the Jews will rebuild their temple and will once again reinstate animal sacrifice at the start of the Tribulation period.

There is an interesting passage in **Isaiah 66:3** that seems to be speaking about the sacrifices made in the Tribulation Temple.

In this passage, Isaiah is talking about a Temple whose sacrifices are not pleasing to God. The sacrifices are as if "swine's blood" had been offered. Jews who reject the sacrifice of Jesus will build the Tribulation Temple, probably with the permission of the antichrist. These sacrifices with not be accepted by God because animal sacrifice is no longer needed since the ultimate sacrifice, that of Jesus the Messiah, has been given. [36]

The movement in Israel to rebuild the Temple is set. The only thing lacking now is the permission to do it, which will probably cause a major war. That war could be the Russian invasion of Israel prophesied in Ezekiel 38 and 39. This will be the seventh event that must happen before the start of the Tribulation.

Copy and paste the code into your web browser for a you tube video on this section: http://www.youtube.com/watch?v=oyWczz QGOMY

---

[36] Arnold Fruchtenbaum, Footsteps of the Messiah (Ariel Ministries 2003), p. 137-18.

Israel, Islam, and Nuclear Bombs

Yom Kippur, the Day of Atonement, is the most holy day in the Jewish year. On this day, Jews around the world will fast for a period of 24 hours. It was on this day in 1973 that a number of Arab states attacked Israel. They attacked at a time when they knew the Israeli soldiers would be the weakest from fasting. Their goal was to drive the Jews into the sea.

Israel came very close to losing that war. So close, in fact, that she was preparing to exercise what is known as the "Samson Option." Sometime after being captured, Samson was brought to the temple of Dagon where he determined to kill himself along with the enemies of Israel by pushing the supporting pillars until the temple collapsed. Thus, the Samson Option is the decision that if Israel is losing, the nation will destroy itself, if that action will also destroy all the invading Arab armies.

Israel's Samson Option is nuclear weapons.[37] Israel had nuclear bombs loaded and ready to use during this war. Fortunately she went on to win this war and a major nuclear war was averted. The Arabs came to realize the only way they could defeat Israel was with nuclear bombs of their own.

It was shortly after the Yom Kippur war, that a man by the name of Saddam Hussein began to build a nuclear reactor just outside Bagdad, Iraq. The first step in the production of nuclear weapons is the building of an operational nuclear reactor. Since Iraq had very large oil fields to provide gas for power plants, Saddam's purpose for building a nuclear power plant was for the eventual destruction of the nation of Israel.

Israel could not allow this to continue. In 1981, shortly before Saddam's nuclear reactor was about to go operational, Israel sent several F-16's into Baghdad. In just two minutes the Israeli fighter jets completely destroyed Saddam's lone

---

[37] Seymour Hersh, "The Samson Option" (Random House 1991).

reactor.[38]

As this was happening, another Islamic country across the eastern border from Iraq, by the name of Iran, saw how easy it was for Israel to take out Saddam's lone reactor. Iran determined to spread out their nuclear production facilities across the entire country. They began to build. Currently Iran is building, at breakneck speed, several reactors, one of which is located under beautiful luxury homes.

Israel cannot allow Iran to go nuclear. In 2005, Israel purchased from America 100 bunker busting bombs, in order to take out Iran's nuclear program.[39] Israel has also developed war games to simulate a mock invasion of Iran. Iran knows that Israel is going to attempt to destroy their nuclear reactors, as they did Saddam's. Iran has publicly warned Israel that if Israel tries to do this, Iran will hit back. This could start a major war in the Middle East that could affect the whole world.

Ezekiel 38:1-7, in the Bible, speaks of a major war involving Russia, and Iran (Persia) prior to the start of the seven year

---

[38] Uri Bar-Joseph, "Two Minutes Over Baghad," (Routledge; second edition (May 30, 2003).
[39]

http://www.usatoday.com/news/world/2005-04-28-israel-bombs_x.html.

Tribulation period spoken of in the book of Revelation. Russia is one of the main allies of Iran. Therefore an attack by Israel on Iran could trigger this great end time battle.

In this prophecy, God tells Ezekiel to prophesy against, "the land of Magog." When Ezekiel wrote this prophecy some 3,600 years ago there was not a land called "Russia." Today's modern Russia is "the land of Magog." [40]

As the Russian army comes against Israel they do not come alone. "Persia" comes with them. Persia is Iran, and, in fact, Iran was called Persia up until 1935.[41] Some of the other nations are difficult to identify, but one is clear and that is Iran.

Ezekiel 38:8

This verse gives us four time factors as to when this great battle will take place:
1. "In the latter years." This battle will not take place in the days of Ezekiel. It will take place in the distant future.
2. When the land of Israel has been "restored from the sword." The Jews living in the land of Israel escaped the sword of Hitler's holocaust.
3. When the Jews have returned back to the land "from many nations." This could not be said of the Jewish return from the Babylonian captivity when they returned

---

[40] Arnold Fruchtenbaum, Footsteps of the Messiah (Ariel Ministries 2003), p. 107.
[41] http://en.wikipedia.org/wiki/Iran.

from only one country. Today, the Jewish people have returned back to their homeland from over 100 different countries.
4. At a time when they are "living securely." This is a perfect description of Israel today. Even though their security may appear to be questionable, the Israelis are among their own people and feel greater security living there than among the other nations of the world.

Ezekiel 38:11 also tells us something about the timing of this battle. When Ezekiel wrote this he must have been scratching his head and thinking, "Wait a minute Lord, are you sure, unwalled villages?" because in the days of Ezekiel every city had a wall around it. No city was safe without a wall.

This is, however, a perfect description of Israel today. Not one city has a wall around it, with the exception of the old city section of Jerusalem. The security fence Israel has built does not encompass any city, but rather protects the borders. This is a perfect description of the land of Israel today.

Ezekiel 38:12 explains Russia's motivation for invading the land of Israel. It is all about money. And it usually is, isn't it. But what does Israel have that Russia would want? Some have pointed to the Dead Sea. The mineral wealth of the Dead Sea is estimated at over 1 trillion dollars. [42] Much of the mineral wealth there can be used for fertilizing crops. This would solve one of Russia's recurring problems, which is how to feed its people. Israel is considered the silicon valley of the Middle East. It is a highly technological state that is constantly making new discoveries and innovations in technology. For whatever reason, **Ezekiel 38:16** foresees Russia and the invading armies covering the land like a cloud.

Ezekiel 38:18-23 It is then that the anger of the Lord is aroused and he causes a great earthquake in the land, so that much of the earth is shaken. This apparently causes some confusion among these invading armies as they begin to fight against each other. (Every man's sword will be against his brother.) Then God will pour upon these armies a torrential rain mixed with hailstones, fire and brimstone, which will completely wipe out them out. Afterward, Israel will realize there really is a God, for only God Himself could send the elements to fight with, and win, this war for them. This does not mean they will become believers in Jesus. Later, at the end of the seven year Tribulation, they will recognize Jesus as the Messiah. But at this point they will become theists. Many Jewish people

---

42

http://www.en.wikipedia.org/wiki/Dead_Sea

.

today, especially in Israel, are atheists or agnostics. In fact, about 25% of Israelis doubt the existence of God. [43] But after this miraculous, great battle, ALL Jewish people will believe in God.

Ezekiel 39:4 There was a tract written years ago with the picture of a vulture on the front of it. The tract claimed that the vultures in Israel were beginning to lay more eggs and to breed more offspring in preparation for this great battle. There is no evidence of this, however, Israel is a natural migratory route for millions of birds each spring and fall as they migrate between Africa and Asia Minor. At sometime in the near future the predatory birds and the beasts of the field will have a feast of Biblical proportions!

Finally, **Ezekiel 39:9** provides another clue as to the timing of this great battle. this battle is so big it takes seven years to clean it up. This battle must take place shortly before the start of the seven year Tribulation since the prophets give us a description of the land of Israel during the millennium as being like the **Garden of Eden**. (**Ezekiel 36:35, Ezekiel 34:13,14, Jeremiah 31:12, Isaiah 51:3**) Dead bodies and burned out tanks do not enhance the beauty of the Garden of Eden. This battle

---

43

http://www.adherents.com/largecom/com_atheist.html.

will be cleaned up before Jesus returns at the end of the seven year tribulation. As Iran is closer and closer to a nuclear bomb, the start of this great battle of Gog and Magog is at the very door.

Copy and paste the code to your web browser for a you tube video on this section: http://www.youtube.com/watch?v=qZqcJVZU9e0

The Tribulation

Revelation 6:1, 2 The Lamb in this Scripture is Jesus, the Lamb of God. (See John 1:29) Therefore this rider on the white horse is not Jesus. While it is true that when Jesus returns he will be riding a white horse, (Rev. 19:11) He will have a sword and not a bow, and He will be wearing a "diadem" crown, not the "steffanos" crown this rider wears.

It is clear that the rider is trying to imitate Jesus. He is identified as the false messiah, or antichrist. The seven years of the Tribulation period starts with the arrival of the antichrist and the signing of his covenant with Israel. (Daniel 9:27)

Revelation 6:3-6 The red horse marks the beginning of the time of war in the Tribulation. While there is peace in the land of Israel as this time, since the covenant of peace has just been signed, yet war breaks out in other parts of the world.

The black horse brings famine. A "measure of wheat" was about the size of a loaf of bread. A "penny" at that time was a day's wage. Because of the severe famine during the Tribulation it will take a day's wage to buy a loaf of bread.

Revelation 6:7, 8 The fourth horse brings death to one fourth of the population of the world. Today that would be just over **one billion** people. To put that in perspective, during World War two, the greatest war the world has known to this point, about sixty million people were killed over a twelve year period. In the Tribulation, about twenty times that many are killed at this point. By the mid-point of the Tribulation, half of the population of the world will have died. It boggles the mind.

Revelation 6:9-11 John sees those who have been killed for their faith in Jesus during the Tribulation. The anti-Christ will be the one instigating this because of his hatred of Jesus and his followers. Those people under the altar are praising the Lamb in the next chapter.

Revelation 6:12-17 Here is the first of several "black-outs" during the Tribulation. It is clear that the people on earth perceive (and rightly so) these judgments as being inflicted on them by God himself. But, rather than repent of their evil deeds, they would rather hide themselves from God, as Adam and Eve hid among the trees in the garden when they committed the first sin again God.

Copy and paste the code to your web browser for a you tube video on this section: http://www.youtube.com/watch?v=ARCSzY Un2d4

Revelation 7:1-8 This is looking back to the beginning of the Tribulation. Notice he says, "hurt not the earth, neither the sea, nor the trees, till we have sealed the servants of our God in their foreheads." This indicates that the sealing of the 144,000 will take place sometime early in the Tribulation, before the horrors of the Tribulation have begun. They are sealed for protection from the trials of the Tribulation. They are sealed for service for God during the Tribulation. They will be God's witnesses during these seven years. Since all true believers in Jesus have already been taken up in the Rapture some time before the start of the Tribulation, God will use the 144,000 as His witnesses during the Tribulation. God always has his witnesses here on earth to testify of His truth.

There has been a lot of speculation as to the identity of the 144,000. Jehovah Witnesses like to think that the most dedicated 144,000 of their cult is the 144,000. Those evangelical Christians who think the church is going to go through the Tribulation think that the Church is really the 144,000. This is based on the idea that the tribe of Dan is missing from the list of the twelve tribes of Israel given here. The reasoning given is "the usual list" of the tribes of Israel is not given here, so it must not be talking about Israel.

A search of the Bible reveals that the

twelve tribes of Israel are listed in the Old Testament over 40 times. **Not one time** is the list of tribes ever given in the same order. There is no "usual list" of tribes in the Bible.

Furthermore, in Deuteronomy 33, the tribe of Simeon is left out of the list of the twelve tribes. Actually, the tribe of Dan is included later in the list of tribes given for the millennium.

Why is there a discrepancy? There is significance in the repeated use of numbers in Scripture. Twelve is the number used for governing. Jesus said to his twelve disciples, "You will sit on twelve thrones and govern the twelve tribes of Israel."

Clearly the 144,000 are Jewish men from the twelve tribes of Israel. Even though most Jews today do not know what tribe they are from, God knows. He will hand pick 12,000 from each tribe to be his witnesses during the Tribulation.

Copy and paste the code to see a video clip of this section on my you tube site at: http://www.youtube.com/watch?v=2JW5om 3bczY

Revelation 7:9-17 After John sees the 144,000, he then sees a "great multitude, which no man could number, of all nations…." These are clearly not Jewish people in contrast to the 144,000. Who are these people? These are people who have come to faith in Jesus during the Tribulation. How did they come to faith? It was through the witness of the 144,000. It is interesting that their number was so great John could not count them, but called them a great multitude.

Later in the book of Revelation John is going to see an army of 200 million. It is estimated there are approximately 200 million believers in Jesus in the world today. Sadly, it has taken almost 2,000 years to arrive at that number.

In the seven years of the Tribulation many more than 200 million people could come to faith in Jesus. Who knows? Perhaps a billion people come to faith, mainly through the witness of the 144,000 sealed Jewish evangelists.

After almost two thousand years of rebelling against the truth that Jesus is the Messiah, the Jewish people will finally "get it right" and once again be used in a mighty way to lead millions to faith in Jesus.

Revelation 8:1-6 There is silence in heaven because of the severity of the plagues that are about to be poured out on the earth. So far the seven seals, which included the four horses, have destroyed a quarter of the earth's population and brought famine and disease.

As the Tribulation progresses, the plagues will increase in severity and intensity. It is compared to a woman in labor who is about to give birth to a baby. As the time of birth get closer, a woman's labor pains will intensify and grow closer together. And so it will be during the Tribulation.

The seal plagues were devastating, but the trumpet plagues will now be even more severe and inflict damage not only on mankind, but on nature itself.

Revelation 8:6-13 and Trumpet #1

This trumpet burns up a third of all the trees in the world and all of the green grass. It is hard to imagine such a sight. Every year extensive fires burn in California and they do not burn up one percent of all the trees in the world.

Trumpet #2

John sees "as it were a great mountain burning with fire was cast into the sea." This is probably a description of an asteroid the size of a mountain that will hit earth at this point. Scientists tell us this has happened in the past, and that it is not a matter of "if" but, "when" the next one will hit. Isn't it amazing that the Bible forecasts, almost 2,000 years ago, what scientists believe will one day happen.

Several movies, such as "Deep Impact," have been produced depicting such an event and the horrors that would follow. Were an asteroid the size of a mountain to hit in the Atlantic Ocean (just as an example, for John does not tell us specifically where it would hit), it would cause a tidal wave several hundred feet high that would possibly wipe out the eastern sea coast of the United States. The fallout from such a hit would blacken the sky for months and have a great affect on weather patterns.

Copy and paste the code to see a video clip of this amazing event on my you tube site at: http://www.youtube.com/watch?v=1W8SGjo 18vg

Trumpet #3
This trumpet is similar to the previous one, except that this asteroid seems to be diffused over a large area. It is not confined to the sea, but spreads itself out over a third of the rivers and waters.

Perhaps this will be an asteroid like the one that hit the ocean, but it is shot with a missile and breaks apart. It still turns out to be very devastating. "Wormwood," the name of the star that hits the earth, means poisonous. A third of the waters become "wormwood" and many people die from drinking this poisoned water.

Trumpet #4
This trumpet causes a third of the sun, a third of the moon and a third of the stars to darken or give less light.

Next, three "woe's" are given. The

last three trumpets are known as "woe" trumpets, because they will be even worse, as we shall see in the next chapter.

Revelation 9:1-12 and Trumpet #5 and The First Woe

The "bottomless pit" is a dwelling place of demons. Here they are loosed to torment men who do not have the seal of God in their foreheads. These men obviously do not worship God or have faith in Jesus, the Lamb of God.

These demons appear as locusts. This is not a description of attack helicopters as some have conjectured, since these locusts attack for the purpose of stinging, not killing, people. Their victims will be tormented for five months or one hundred fifty days. The people will be in such pain that they will want to die, but they will not be able to.

The demons have a king over them whose name is given in Hebrew and Greek. It means the same in both languages. It means destroyer.

Revelation 9:13-21 and Trumpet #6

The sixth trumpet brings yet another demonic attack on the earth. This time, instead of tormenting people, they will kill a third of all who live on the face of the earth. The number of this demonic army is "two hundred thousand thousand." In mathematical terms: 200 x 1,000 x 1,000 =

200 million. John says: "I heard the number of them." He is
saying, "Yes, I know this number seems unbelievably high, but I have the number right." At the time John was living, there were not even 200 million people alive in the whole world. Now he says there is going to be one army of 200 million.

He is not speaking here about China. Although China has a 200 million man army, this is clearly a demonic army because they ascend from the earth, from the Euphrates River. As the previous demons ascended from the earth, so do these. Amazingly, after these horrific plagues, men still refuse to repent of their evil ways.

Revelation 10:1-11 and Trumpet #7

The little book the angel has is possibly the title deed to the earth. The sweet taste John experiences probably speaks of the sweetness of God's message for believers. But when he swallows it, it becomes bitter in his stomach, probably speaking of the message of judgment on unbelievers given in God's word.

Revelation 11:1, 2

The Temple spoken of here is the Temple the Jews are prepared to rebuild in Jerusalem. At this point in the book of Revelation the Temple has been rebuilt and the Jews are once again making sacrifices.

The forty-two months is the last half

of the Tribulation. Jerusalem will be under gentile control until the end of the Tribulation. The Jews control Jerusalem now but they will not be able to maintain unbroken control of Jerusalem. They will regain control at the end of the Tribulation when Jesus returns and sets up his kingdom. He will rule and reign for one thousand years from Jerusalem.

Revelation 11:3-6

There has been speculation as to who the two witnesses are. The most common candidates are: Moses and Elijah, or Enoch and Elijah.

The case for Moses and Elijah stems from the fact that the plagues the two witnesses bring upon the earth are similar to the plagues that Moses and Elijah brought in their day. Moses and Elijah also appeared with Jesus on the Mount of Transfiguration, which gives them more credence.

The argument for Enoch and Elijah is based on the fact that they were the only two people in the Old Testament who did not die. Elijah was taken to heaven in a whirlwind, while Hebrews 11:5 states that Enoch was translated into the next life without dying. Hebrews says "it is appointed unto men to die once," and since Elijah and Enoch never died, and the two witnesses will die, it is thought they could be the two witnesses.

However, death is simply a normal event,

not a hard and fast rule. There have been many people who were raised to life and who then died again. They actually died twice. At the Rapture, millions will be translated to heaven without ever dying. In the case of the two witnesses, it is best to see them as modern day Jewish men whom the Lord will empower, just as He empowered Moses and Elijah.

Revelation 11:7-14 and the Second Woe

The two witnesses will prophesy during the first three and a-half years of the Tribulation. The antichrist then kills them in the city of Jerusalem and the whole world is able to see their dead bodies which are left in the street for the next three and a half days.

Before the invention of television it would have been difficult to understand how this prophecy could be accomplished. This will be a major news story and will be shown on worldwide television.

Since it is the antichrist that kills the two witnesses, it will appear that he has more power than God. But, after just three and one half days these two men are resurrected and translated immediately to Heaven in a mini-rapture. Their translation is followed up by an earthquake in which 7,000 people are killed. People give glory to God, in the realization that He is all powerful.

Revelation 11:15-19 and Trumpet #7

People who believe the Rapture will happen in the middle of the Tribulation identify this trumpet as the one announcing the Rapture. But, notice there is no indication of the Rapture happening here. There are no reports of missing people, and no chaos on earth because of millions suddenly disappearing. Why? The Rapture has already taken place prior to the start of the Tribulation.

This seventh trumpet precedes the seven bowl judgments. These will be the final and worst judgments of the Tribulation.

Revelation 12:1-5

Many ideas have been given as to the identity of the woman clothed with the sun, and the moon and on her head a crown of twelve stars. However, the Bible is the best interpreter of itself. Anywhere symbols are used in the Bible their meanings are always given within the text, or in another part of the Bible. Here, the meaning of the "sun, moon and twelve stars" is not given. But these are the same symbols used in one of the dreams Joseph had when he was a young man. (**Genesis 37**) In Joseph's dream, the sun, moon, and stars represented his father, mother, and brothers, who later became the twelve tribes of the nation of Israel.

The woman here represents the nation of Israel. She gives birth to a child.

Verse five says her child will someday rule the world. This is a direct quote of **Psalm2**, which is a Psalm about Jesus, the Messiah. The child here represents Jesus. The woman (Israel) gives birth to the child (Jesus) in verse two. Jesus came to this world via the nation of Israel.

The identity of the dragon is given in verse nine. He is none other than Satan himself. He has seven heads representing seven past kingdoms. He has ten horns representing ten present day kingdoms. The stars of heaven represent the angels. The dragon's tail pulled out a third of the stars of heaven and cast them to earth. . This is a reference to Satan's rebellion against God. One-third of the angels followed Satan in his rebellion against God. They were cast out of Heaven with Satan

Here we get a real sense of the spiritual battle that never ceases between Satan and God. Satan wanted to devour the child (Jesus) of the woman (Israel). But the child (Jesus) was taken up to Heaven by God, showing that the sacrifice of Jesus on the cross and his resurrection defeated Satan's purposeful attempt to overthrow God.

Revelation 12:6

These days are the last half of the Tribulation. The woman (Israel) flees into the wilderness at this time to escape the persecution of the antichrist. The prophet

Micah tells us Israel will flee to a place called Bozrah, better known as Petra. (**Micah 2:12**) Bozrah is the Aramaic name for this place while Petra is the Greek name. Petra is located in the desert in Southern Jordan. It was originally inhabited by the Edomites, who were the descendants of Esau, one of the sons of Isaac. It is a city that was carved of sand stone. There is just one narrow passage leading back into the city. A few people could hold off an entire army at this place, making it the perfect hiding place for Israel during this time. Here at Petra, God will supernaturally provide for Israel during the last half of the Tribulation.

The antichrist has now set up an image of himself in the rebuilt Jewish Temple. Jesus and Daniel, the prophet, both spoke of this image as the abomination of desolation. (**Daniel 9:27, Matthew 24:15**) Jesus urged those of the Jewish people who saw this event to flee into the wilderness. And that is exactly what Israel does at this time as this verse foretells.

Revelation 12:7-12 and The Third Woe

This war in heaven is probably fought in the second heaven. It is the atmosphere around the earth. The third heaven is the home of the saints of God.

Satan is referred to in Scripture as the "prince of the power of the air." Here at the mid-point of the Tribulation, Michael and his angels force Satan down to the earth. Michael is mentioned several times in Scripture, especially in relationship to Israel.

Those on the earth experience a "woe" because Satan himself is now living with them. He knows his time is short. He now has only three and a half more years before he will be defeated by the return of Jesus to earth.

Revelation 12:13-17

Once Satan is cast down to earth he begins to persecute the woman (Israel) who gave birth to the child (Jesus).

Satan is the world's biggest anti-Semite. He hates Israel and the Jewish people because, through them, the Messiah came into the world and secured redemption through the blood He shed on the cross.

God has also made promises to Israel that remain unfulfilled. If Satan can destroy Israel before the return of Jesus, God's plan is defeated. This, however, will never happen.

It is interesting that anti-Semitic groups today usually have some sort of satanic roots. Adolph Hitler and the Nazi's are prime examples. The swastika is the symbol of a broken cross. Hitler was involved in the occult and when he gave his speeches many people noticed how it seemed a strange power came over him like he was demon possessed.

As Satan begins his persecution of

the woman (Israel), she flees into the wilderness (Petra). Here she is cared for during the last half of the Tribulation. A time, times and half a time is another way of saying the last three and a half years of the Tribulation.

The fact that the woman is given two wings of an eagle suggests some sort of Divine intervention to help Israel flee. This same type of language is used during Israel's exodus from Egypt. God miraculously parted the waters of the Red Sea for Israel to walk through on dry land. Pharaoh and his army were drowned while trying to follow them because God allowed the waters to return. In recollection of this great miracle God said to Israel, "I bore you on eagles' wings." (**Exodus 19**)

To stop the woman (Israel) from fleeing, the serpent (Satan) casts a flood out of his mouth. The word "flood" is sometimes used to describe an army. This could be an army Satan sends to destroy Israel as she is fleeing into the wilderness. But, the earth helps the woman (Israel) by opening her mouth and swallowing up the flood (possible army) which the dragon (Satan) cast out of his mouth (commanded to attack).

When Satan sees that Israel has once again escaped from him, he is very angry and begins to persecute and kill others who keep the commands of God and the testimony of Jesus. He will kill millions of those who have come to faith in Jesus through the witness of the 144,000 Jewish evangelists mentioned in Revelation chapter seven. The souls of those who were martyred by the antichrist are mentioned in chapter six, verse nine, as being under the altar.

Revelation 13:1-2

The "sea" in the Bible, when used symbolically, represents gentile nations. When John says he saw the beast (antichrist) rising out of the sea, this indicates the antichrist will be a gentile (not Jewish) and will arise out of the gentile nations, not Israel.

The seven heads represent seven past kingdoms and the ten horns are ten present day kingdoms. The leopard, bear, and lion refer back to a vision Daniel had in chapter seven of his book. He saw these same animals in his vision and they represent the following kingdoms: Lion = Babylon, Bear = Medes-Persians, Leopard = Greece.

The kingdom of the beast (antichrist) will take on the characteristics of these three kingdoms. The beast (antichrist) is empowered by the dragon, which chapter twelve identifies as Satan.

Revelation 13:3-10

This is the mid-point of the Tribulation. The beast (antichrist) is somehow killed. The expression, "as it were wounded to death," is an idiom for death and resurrection. The same idiom is used of Jesus in Revelation 5:6 where it says the Lamb (Jesus) stood "as if it had been slain." We know that Jesus died and was then resurrected on the third day.

At some time after the death of the antichrist, he will be raised back to life, apparently through the power of Satan who is empowering the beast (antichrist). This is all allowed by God and is part of the great deception during the Tribulation. Since the antichrist comes back to life, people begin to worship him and realize it is futile to fight against him. He blasphemes God and continues to rule forty-two months, which is the last half of the Tribulation. His rule is now worldwide in that he has power over "all" nations. All who have not put their faith in Jesus at this point of the Tribulation will begin to worship the antichrist. He will persecute and kill all those who do not worship him.

Millions of those who have come to faith in Jesus through the witness of the 144,000 will now be martyred for their faith.

The "Lamb's Book of Life" should be distinguished from the "Book of Life." **Psalm 69:28** speaks of the Book of Life, in which the name of everyone who has ever lived is written. When someone is born, his or her name is written in the "Book of Life." It appears that only believer's names will be written in the "Lamb's Book of Life." The Scripture speaks of people's names being blotted out of the "Book of Life." If a person dies as an unbeliever, his or her name is then blotted out of the "Book of Life." However, when a person becomes a believer in Jesus, his or her name is then written into the "Lamb's Book of Life." **(Revelation 21:27)**

Revelation 13:11-18

This second beast is known as "the false prophet." The fact that he comes out of the earth, or land, suggests he will be Jewish. That he looks "like a lamb" indicates he will be a false messiah, counterfeiting the work of Jesus, the true "Lamb of God." His horns represent power. While the false prophet has the same powers as the antichrist, he does not focus attention upon himself. Rather the false prophet causes worship of the beast (antichrist), which has just risen from the dead. The false prophet at this point sets up an image of the beast (antichrist). We know from other Scripture that this will be set-up in the rebuilt Jewish Temple in Jerusalem. **(Daniel 9:27, Matthew23:15, 1 Thessalonians 2:4)**

The false prophet also has power to miraculously cause the image of the beast to speak! The message of the false prophet is to worship the antichrist, whose image is able to also perform miracles. These miracles are done through the power of Satan.

People may claim they can do miracles, and attribute the miracle to the power of God. While these can be genuine, it is important to understand that Satan also has power and is able to do great miracles. Because someone is able to perform a "miracle," does not necessarily mean it is done through the power of God. When discerning whether the miracle is from God or not, the message of the person should be considered along with the miracle. The false prophet then institutes what is known as, "the mark of the beast." It is the number 666 placed on the right hand or forehead.

For the last half of the tribulation, people will not be able to buy or sell anything (at least legally) unless they have this mark. Even today governments and businesses are experimenting with this type of buying and selling. For years now computer chips have been implanted under the skin of dogs and cats to help identify them. It is popular in Europe for young people to get "chipped," that is, to have a RFID (radio frequency identification) computer chip the size of a grain of rice implanted under their skin. It is usually implanted in their right hand.

Retina eye scans are also becoming a popular form of identification. The technology is here and is already being implemented. This indicates that the start of the Tribulation must be very close, especially since the mark of the beast is not instituted until the mid-point of the Tribulation.

The number six is the number of man. God created man on the sixth day of creation. Three sixes is an exaltation of man over God. It is man rebelling against God. In Hebrew and Greek, each letter of the alphabet has a numerical equivalent. For instance, A = 1, B = 2, C = 3, etc. J = 10, K = 20, T = 100 etc. Each person's name will have a numerical value. The numerical value of the name of the antichrist will add up to 666. People who are alive at this time, who have wisdom and discernment, will be able to know the identity of the anti-Christ by adding up the letters of his name.

About one in every 25,000 names will add up to 666. Because someone's name adds up to that number, it does not mean he is the anti-Christ. He will also have to be in a position of power and give himself over to the control of Satan.

Copy and paste the code in your web browser to see a video clip of the "mark of the beast" technology on my you tube site: http://www.youtube.com/watch?v=hP2SXP 685fw

Revelation 14:1-5

This is an interlude in the book. At the point when it seems as if all is going in favor of Satan and the antichrist, the 144,000 are seen standing in victory with Jesus. A friendly reminder that in the end, Jesus will be victorious!

There is more information here about the 144,000 that was not given in Revelation chapter 7. They are all unmarried men since they are "not defiled with women," but are called "virgins." They have never had any sexual relationship with women. There is a sense in which the sexual relationship, even within the bonds of marriage, is a defiling thing. Before God gave the Law to Israel, He instructed the people not to have any sexual relations on the day before. (**Exodus 19:15**)

Another example from the Old Testament is when King Saul was trying to kill David. In his haste to flee, David went into the Tabernacle and took some of the bread that is only lawful for the Priests to eat. The Priest said David could take this bread and feed his men with it under one condition: "if the young men have kept themselves from women." (**I Samuel 21:4**) The 144,000 will be totally pure in that sense. They also are the "first fruits" of the Tribulation. They will be the first ones to come to faith in Jesus during the Tribulation. This will happen at the very beginning of the Tribulation. They will lead millions of people to faith in Jesus during this time. Because of their faithfulness, they are given a special song which only they can learn. They are "without fault and guile," which means that their sins have been washed in the blood of the Lamb.

Revelation 14:6-7 Apparently people on earth will be able to see this angel flying through the sky admonishing them not to worship the antichrist, but to give glory to God. It seems God is giving unbelievers in the Tribulation an extra special message because of the supernatural signs of deception the anti-Christ is able to perform.

Revelation 14:8-11 The fall of Babylon is discussed in chapter 18. Suffice it to say that at this point, it is now the headquarters of the antichrist and this second angel is prophetically informing people of the fall of the antichrist's kingdom.

The third angel warns people of the price for taking 666, the mark of the beast, in their right hand or forehead. By taking the mark people might be able to buy and sell things for the remaining three and a half years of the Tribulation, but if they take the mark they will for all eternity be suffering torment in the lake of fire.

Revelation 14:12-13 The saints will be between a rock and a hard place. It is far better to put your faith in Jesus and be killed for your faith, than to take the mark of the beast and spend eternity in the lake of fire.

Revelation 14:14-16 The one "like unto the son of man" is Jesus Himself. The phrase, "son of man" is a Messianic title and one that Jesus frequently used of himself. "Reaping" is a common term for salvation. Jesus told his disciples to look for a harvest of souls. (**John 4:35, 36**) This is a reference to the millions who will come to faith during the Tribulation.

Revelation 14:17-20 Treading the winepress is a symbol of judgment. This speaks of the unbelievers who will be killed during the Tribulation. Their blood flows out of the city (Jerusalem) 1,600 furlongs, which is approximately 200 miles. This is about the distance from Jerusalem to Petra, where the Jews will be hiding during the last half of the Tribulation. More will be said about this in chapter 19.

Revelation 15:1-8 This chapter is a prelude to the final seven plagues of the Tribulation. The song of Moses can be found in Exodus chapter 15. It is a song of deliverance. Moses, through the power of God, delivered Israel from the plagues in Egypt. The redeemed are now viewed in heaven, delivered from eternal punishment in the lake of fire.

The seven bowl judgments that are about to be poured out on earth, will be the worst judgments of the Tribulation. They will completely devastate the earth. Jesus said if the Tribulation were allowed to go on much longer, no one would survive. **(Matthew 24:22)**

Revelation 16:1, 2 and Bowl #1 As the first bowl is poured out, only those who have taken the mark of the beast are affected. "Grievous sores" come upon them. It is just a foretaste of what awaits them in the lake of fire. This is reminiscent of the plagues God poured out on Egypt in the days of Moses. At that time, God also made a distinction between the Israelites and the Egyptians, in that some of the plagues only affected the Egyptians and not the Israelites.

Revelation 16:3 and Bowl#2 Earlier in the trumpet judgments, a third of the sea had been turned to blood. Here at the end of the Tribulation, the whole sea is turned to blood.

Revelation 16:4-7 and Bowl #3 Now all of the rivers and fountains of waters are turned to blood. Since man has been so blood thirsty and murderous in killing those who have come to faith in Jesus during the Tribulation, men are given blood to drink. Lest it seem the judgment of God is over harsh, an angel proclaims, "True and righteous are thy judgments."

Revelation 16:8, 9 and Bowl #4 As people are scorched by the sun, they still refuse to repent. On the contrary they lash out in blasphemy against their Creator.

Revelation 16:10, 11 and Bowl #5

The "seat" or throne or headquarters of the beast is in Babylon. Babylon is covered in darkness, and in chapter 18 the headquarters of the antichrist will fall, never to rise again.

Revelation 16:12-16 and Bowl #6

At this point the Euphrates River, which separates the East from the West, is dried up to allow the kings of the East easy access to the final battle of the Tribulation, the battle of Armageddon.

The headwaters of the Euphrates begin in the country of Turkey. Over the last few decades, Turkey has built a series of over twenty dams on the Euphrates with which Turkey could shut off the flow of water just like a water faucet is turned off. The water being "dried up" could be the result of a "water war" in that part of the world. Since the preceding trumpets turned the water to blood, clean fresh water will be at a premium. The kings of the East could be a reference to China, but more likely refers to the armies of the antichrist, who will now lure all the nations of the world to Israel and the battle of Armageddon. This will be Satan's last ditch attempt to destroy Israel, God's chosen people. It will be Satan's undoing.

Revelation 16:17-21 and Bowl #7

"It is done." This is the final judgment of the Tribulation, and it is a devastating one. An earthquake hits the "great city" which is Jerusalem, and it is divided into three parts. This appears to be the strongest earthquake to ever have occurred as every city in the world is impacted. Skyscrapers around the world will topple over. To make matters worse, 100 pound hail stones begin falling from the sky which will completely flatten every city and building on earth and kill millions of people.

Revelation 17:1, 2 Chapter 17 speaks of the fall of religious Babylon, while chapter 18 will deal with the fall of economic Babylon.

The harlot represents the false religious system setup during the Tribulation. It will be a uniting of the major world religions. A "harlot" or "prostitute" sells her body for money. Here, the harlot will sell religion for financial gain.

"Waters" many times in the Bible symbolizes gentile nations. The fact that Babylon sits on many waters would signify she has power and influence over many nations.

"Kings" committing fornication with her speaks of a unity between church and state. During the Tribulation, the church and state will join forces to not only extort money from people, but to persecute and kill true believers in Jesus. (v.6)

Revelation 17:3-6 The color **red** could symbolize the blood this church/state religious system will shed. "Beasts" many times represents kingdoms in Scripture. The fact that the harlot is riding the beast tells us the kingdom of the antichrist will empower the one world religion that is set up in the Tribulation. Seven heads represents six past kingdoms plus one present kingdom, while the ten horns represent the ten kings that rule in the Tribulation.

The woman is dressed in very expensive clothing and jewelry indicating that she is selling religion for financial gain; this is the main reason she is religious. It was an ancient custom for prostitutes to write their name on their forehead. The harlot's name is "Mystery Babylon the great, the mother of harlots and abominations of the earth."

The use of the word "mystery" in the New Testament has the idea of a new teaching not found in the Old Testament. There are eight mysteries in the New Testament and this is one of them. Dr. Arnold Fruchtenbaum puts it well in his radio manuscript on The Eight Mysteries of the New Testament:

"The mystery is not Babylon, nor is the mystery the fact that Babylon was the originator and center of idolatry; this is already known from the Old Testament. The mystery is the fact that Babylon will develop into a one-world unified religion, and will

rule the world religiously for the first half of the tribulation: it will be headquartered and based in the city of Babylon; it will be supported by the governments of that day; and, it will be the primary persecutor of believers who will not submit to its religious authority. All of this was totally unrevealed in the Old Testament."

Many Bible scholars believe that the Babylon John is writing about here is actually a code name for Rome. They base this on the fact that Rome has been a major persecutor of believers in the past and even today when the <u>Roman</u> Catholic Church's persecution of evangelical believers for the past thousand plus years is taken into account.

Babylon is also thought to be Rome because verse nine says the harlot sets on seven mountains, and Rome is a city set on seven hills.

There are however, several problems with this view. First, nowhere else in Scripture is Babylon equated with Rome. Babylon was a major city in John's day with a larger Jewish population than Rome. The Jews, some 600 years earlier, went into captivity in Babylon. When John writes Babylon, there would be no reason for a Jewish person to think John was talking about Rome.

What about the seven mountains John mentioned in verse nine? The seven mountains are used in a symbolic sense, which is brought out in verse ten where the mountains are equated with kings. John adds that five of the kings have fallen. If these were literal mountains in the city of Rome, we would expect that five of the mountains of Rome would have fallen, but they have not.

The harlot, religious Babylon, which is the one world religion of the Tribulation, will be the main persecutor of true believers in Jesus. Millions of people will come to faith in Jesus. The antichrist and his one world religion will kill them. The martyrdom of believers is shown in chapter six.

There is some debate over the seven kingdoms. This is a possible breakdown:
1. Tarquin Kings 753-510 BC
2. Counsulors 510-494 BC
3. Dictators 494-390 BC
4. Republicans 390-59 BC
5. Triumvirate 59-27 BC
6. Imperialism 27 BC to Present
7. The Anti-Christ

The one that is yet to come will be the kingdom of the antichrist. In verse eleven, the beast that was and is not, is a reference to the death of the antichrist. He is the eighth king, in that he subdued three of the ten original kings, making him the eighth king of the One World Government. But, he is of the seventh kingdom in that his kingdom is the seventh kingdom of the Roman Empire to be set up.

The ten kings of verse twelve are the future ten kings of the One World Government that will be set up in the end times. Notice, they do not have a kingdom yet. This indicates that the prophecies in the book of Revelation will be fulfilled in the future.

The ten kings of the One World Government will give their power and allegiance to the beast who is the anti-Christ.

Revelation 17:7-15 The beast ascending out of the bottomless pit is a reference to the resurrection of the antichrist from the dead. At the mid-point of the Tribulation, the beast will be killed (13:4), but will then be raised back to life. This is to counterfeit the miracle of the resurrection of Jesus to make the false Christ look like the real Christ. Those who see this great miracle take place will be amazed and many will even worship the antichrist as he proclaims himself as God.

Revelation 17:16-18 The ten horns are the ten final world kingdoms. At the beginning of the Tribulation they work with the "harlot," the one-world false religious system, to control the people of the world. At the mid-point of the Tribulation they turn against the one-world religion and begin to persecute it. They set up their own religion, which will be the worship of the antichrist as a god.

Revelation 18:1, 2 The Tribulation is finally coming to an end after seven long years. Babylon has been the headquarters of the antichrist during the Tribulation and it is now time for God to pass judgment on this city. It will not be the first time God has judged Babylon for its sin. Babylon is one of the oldest cities in the world. She is first mentioned in the Bible in Genesis chapter nine as the place where the Tower of Babel is being built. "Babylon" and "Babel" are the same place. Here, at the end of the Tribulation, Babylon, which is the headquarters of the anti-Christ, is destroyed. It will remain desolate even through the thousand-year reign of Christ on earth when Jesus will set up his kingdom and rule and reign over the earth for 1,000 years. This is known as the "millennial reign of Christ." During these thousand years, the earth will be transformed into a paradise as it was in the beginning when God first created it.

But, as the world is renewed, Babylon will remain desolate even through the thousand-year kingdom. It will be a habitation for demons. The reason is given in the next verse.

Revelation 18:3-8 Amazingly there are still people of the Lord who are somehow able to be living in Babylon even up to the day of her destruction. They will be living in hidden places as the antichrist will seek to kill any and all who refuse to take his mark and worship him as God.

Revelation 18:9-11 Three groups will mourn over the destruction of Babylon; kings, merchants and sailors, for they were the ones profiting from her merchandise.

Revelation 18:12-14 Twenty-eight items are listed here which represent anything a person could possibly buy or sell.

Revelation 18:15-18 While Babylon today is not a great city, it will become so during the Tribulation period. There is a prophecy in Zechariah five that indicates Babylon will rise to power very quickly, almost overnight.

Zechariah 5:5-11 An "ephah" is about the size of a bushel basket and represents the standard of an economy. Back in Bible times, when people went to the market they would measure out grain in an ephah. The woman sitting in this basket represents wickedness, speaking of financial fraud. Then, two women with the wings of a stork pick up the ephah and carry it to the "land of Shinar." A stork was an unclean animal according to the Old Testament law. (**Leviticus 11:19**) The fact that they have wings suggests this will happen very quickly, almost overnight. The "land of Shinar" is the same place as Babylon.

The economic standard of the world will shift very quickly to Babylon. At this time, New York City is one of the main economic centers of the world. This will change in the last days from New York to Babylon.

If New York is destroyed in a major war, then certainly the world will have to look for a new place to center world trade. According to this prophecy, the economic center of the world will eventually become Babylon. In order for Babylon to fall, it must first rise.

Revelation 18:19-20 Three groups of people mourn over the destruction of Babylon, and three groups of people will rejoice over her destruction. The "heaven" is probably a reference to the angels, the holy apostles and prophets.

Revelation 18:21-24 He confirms that Babylon will remain desolate, even through the millennial reign of Christ because of her "sorceries." It is the Greek word, "pharmakeia" referring to drug use, and as drugs are also used in sorcery and worship of Satan.

Babylon's fall is also because she shed the blood of the prophets and saints and took advantage of all people.

Copy and paste the code to your web browser to see a video on this section from my you tube site:

http://www.youtube.com/watch?v=WLM40l
8mGmA

Revelation 19:1-4 As the Saints see
the destruction of Babylon they rejoice and
give glory to God for bringing her to justice.
The four and twenty elders probably
represent the Church in Heaven giving glory
to God Almighty.

Revelation 19:5-9 Prior to the
return of Jesus to earth at the end of the
seven year Tribulation the Bride of Christ is
made ready. According to **2 Corinthians
11:2, 3**, the Church is the Bride of Christ.
Here the Church, which is made up of
believers in Jesus, is arrayed in fine linen
which tells us the judgment seat of Christ
has already taken place. (**2 Corinthians
5:10**)

Revelation 19:10 It is sad that many
Christians today shy away from the study of
Bible prophecy and some even discourage it.
Here we see the importance of Bible
prophecy. It is testifying of Jesus!

Revelation 19:11-16 The rider on
the white horse is none other than Jesus
himself. In Revelation 6:2 the antichrist was
riding on a white horse as a cheap imitation
of the real Jesus. The real Jesus is here,
returning to defeat the armies of the
antichrist at the battle of Armageddon. (War
is sometimes necessary.) The armies of
heaven who are following him are the angels

and church saints who are now in Heaven. A sharp sword goes out of his mouth which is a figure of speech telling us that just as God spoke the world into existence so he will defeat the anti-Christ by simply speaking the word. (**2 Thessalonians 2:8**)

Revelation 19:17-19 As in the battle of Gog and Magog in **Ezekiel 39**, the birds of the air are encouraged to gather for a great feast of human flesh. In the meantime the antichrist gathers his army in a last ditch attempt to make a war with Jesus when he returns. His armies are gathered to a place called Armageddon, according to **Revelation 16:16**. In the beginning of this war it appears the antichrist is successful. According to **Zechariah 14:2** he is able to take the city of Jerusalem. When it looks like all hope is lost, and when it looks like Israel will be destroyed, Jesus returns in all of his power and glory and defeats the antichrist with a single spoken word!

Revelation 19:20-21 Once the beast (or antichrist) and the false prophet are slain, they are immediately cast into the lake of fire. They are the first to be cast into this terrifying place but they won't be the last. One thousand years later Satan will be joining them along with other unbelievers. (chapter 20)

Revelation 20:1-3 The angel who binds Satan is not identified, but it is the first time in Scripture Satan is said to be "bound" despite the fact that many Christians attempt to bind Satan with their prayers.

He is cast into the abyss, which is in the center of the earth. This is only a temporary holding place for him, as he will be released at the end of the 1,000 year reign of Christ.

Revelation 20:4-6 Finally the saints are seen reigning and ruling with Jesus in his Kingdom. As Jesus said to his twelve disciples in **Matthew 19:28.**

After Jesus returns to earth, defeats the anti-Christ and saves Israel, there will be a seventy-five day interlude **(Daniel 12:11, 12)** before the millennial reign of Christ begins. During this interlude the judgment of the nations will take place, as well as the marriage supper of the Lamb. Jesus spoke of this marriage feast in **Matthew 25:1-13.** The judgment of the nations is found in **Matthew 25:31-46.** In this Scripture the sheep (believers) are separated from the goats (unbelievers).

After the seventy-five day interlude the reign of Christ will begin. Jesus will rule on the throne of David from Jerusalem, Israel. This is based on the promise God made to King David in **2 Samuel 7:12-17**, known as the Davidic Covenant. (**Zechariah 14:8-21, Luke 1:32, 33**)

Great topographical changes will take place in Israel as the Mountain of the Lord will be high and lifted up. (**Isaiah 2:1-**

5). **Ezekiel 40-48** gives a detailed description of the Mountain of the Lord, the tribes of Israel, and the rebuilt Temple during the millennium. The Mountain of the Lord itself will be approximately fifty miles by fifty miles. The city of Jerusalem will sit atop the mount and will be roughly ten miles square.

The millennial Temple will also sit atop the mount and will be one square mile. What will be the purpose of a Temple since sacrifices are no longer needed? Jesus, the Lamb of God, has already given the perfect sacrifice. It appears the millennial sacrifices will simply be a memorial of the sacrifice of Jesus. As the Old Testament sacrifices pointed forward to the coming sacrifice of Jesus, the millennial sacrifices will look back as a reminder of the sacrifice He gave on the cross, much like communion reminds us of his death, burial and resurrection.

A river will flow from the Temple in Jerusalem to the west into the Mediterranean Sea and to the East into the Dead Sea. It will heal the waters of the Dead Sea. (**Ezekiel 47:1-12**)

Today the Dead Sea is the lowest spot on earth sinking some 1,300 feet below sea level. By comparison, Death Valley, the lowest spot in America, is only around 200 feet below sea level. The Dead Sea is also the saltiest sea, ten times saltier than any other ocean. It is so salty no fish can live in it. All that will change during the millennial reign of Christ.

During the mid 1980's the government of Israel had a plan to dig a canal from the Mediterranean Sea to the Dead Sea to help raise the water level in the Dead Sea as the water was slowly being used up. The Lord will do this for them during the millennium!

War and crime, sickness and disease will be virtually unknown during the millennial reign of Christ. The earth will be what God originally intended for it to be, and man will live to be hundreds of years old as he did prior to the flood of Noah. In fact, **Isaiah 65:20** says that if a man dies at 100 years of age he will be considered just a child as most people will live to be hundreds and hundreds of years. Man's life span is one hundred years for an unbeliever and up to a thousand years for believers.

Isaiah 65:17-25 tells us the earth will be rejuvenated during this time and accounts for the ability of man to once again live to be hundreds of years old. It will be a time of prosperity, longevity of life and security.

Even the animal kingdom will be changed. The wolf, leopard, and lion will lay down with the lamb and "they shall not hurt nor destroy in all my holy mountain says the Lord." (**Isaiah 11:6; 65:18-25**)

The end of the one thousand year

reign of Christ will give way to the final judgment of the lost and the "eternal order" where all believers from all ages will live in the New Jerusalem (Heaven) for all eternity. **Revelation 20:7-9** Satan is released from his prison and is allowed to lead a rebellion against Christ. Jesus has been ruling with a rod of iron and life on earth has been like the Garden of Eden.

Yet Satan is still able to convince quite a number of people to turn against Christ.

While this battle is called "Gog and Magog," it is <u>not</u> the same as the "Gog and Magog" battle spoken of in **Ezekiel 38**.

There are quite a number of differences between these two battles. In the Ezekiel battle, specific countries are named. In this battle the whole world is involved. In the Ezekiel battle there are six things that destroy the invading armies, while here it is "fire from heaven" that consumes them. And after the Ezekiel battle there is a seven year clean up period. Here no clean up is mentioned. In fact it is after this that the earth is completely destroyed and a new heaven and new earth are created. Why this battle is called "Gog and Magog" is unclear, but what is clear is that this battle is totally different from Ezekiel 38, 39.

Revelation 20:10 The devil joins the antichrist and the false prophet in the lake of fire where they will be tormented day and night forever. There is no second chance. "Forever" always means "forever" everywhere in Scripture.

Revelation 20:11-15 This is known as "The Great White Throne Judgment." Unbelievers from all the centuries are present at this judgment. Here the lost are judged, but not to see if they will be accepted into heaven. They are all cast into the lake of fire. They are judged to determine their degree of punishment in the lake of fire.

Someone like Adolf Hitler will receive a much greater punishment than someone who lived an average, yet sinful life. The Book of Life is there to show them their name does not appear. They face eternal death, as the Psalmist beseeched the Lord concerning the wicked. **Psalm 69:28**

Billions of lost souls are seen cast into an eternal lake of fire for everlasting punishment. But it all gives way to two of the most glorious chapters in the Bible, a stunning description of Heaven itself.

Revelation 21:1-8 There are two views among Christians about the "new heaven and new earth." Some believe that this present world is simply rejuvenated while others think that this present world will be completely destroyed and a new world will be created.

Heaven is called the "New Jerusalem." Jerusalem means the "City of

Peace." The earthly Jerusalem has seen many wars over the years. The new heavenly Jerusalem will truly live up to its name: "The city of peace!"

When verse four says "He will wipe away all tears from their eyes," it is probably a reference to God wiping away the tears of believers as they see people they know cast into the lake of fire at the Great White Throne Judgment.

Revelation 21:9-17 The measurement of the New Jerusalem is estimated to be 1,500 miles long, wide, and high. That is a city of unbelievable size. No city today or throughout history, compares to this city, the New Jerusalem. It is 30 times larger than Chicago and its surrounding suburbs. The highest building in Chicago is just over 100 stories high. The New Jerusalem is some 1,500 miles high! Literally billions upon billions of people could live in this great city with plenty of room to spare.

Revelation 21:18-27 The precious stones used in the foundation of the city have been compared to the stones on the breast plate of the High Priest of Israel. They are similar but not exactly the same.

No Temple is needed in the city because God Himself dwells there. Only those whose names are in the "Lamb's Book of Life" may enter the city. And a person's name is entered into the Lamb's Book of

Life when he or she becomes a believer in Jesus.

Revelation 22:1-5 The "Tree of Life" was also in the Garden of Eden in the beginning of creation. After Adam and Eve sinned by partaking of the Tree of Knowledge, the one tree from which God had forbidden them to eat, they were put out of the Garden and access to the Tree of Life was guarded. Perhaps the tree was destroyed in the flood of Noah. Here it reappears, giving healing or "therapy" to all in the city. Since there will be no sickness in Heaven it remains to been seen what the whole function of the tree will be.

Revelation 22:6-17 John is told not to seal up the prophecy, but Daniel was told to "seal up" his prophecy (**Daniel 12:4**). It was not possible to understand Daniel's prophecy since further revelation by God was needed. Now John is given that further revelation and so we are able to understand his prophecy and also Daniel's prophecy.

Revelation 22:18-21 The book of Revelation and the Bible as a whole closes with a warning. Do not take away from it or add to it. Those who do will have no part in heaven, the New Jerusalem. Every cult and false religion will either add to the Bible or take away from the Bible. For example, Judaism takes away from the Scriptures in that the Rabbis only accept the Old

Testament (Tanach) and reject the New Testament. Roman Catholicism adds to the Bible by adding their catechisms and extra-Biblical books. Mormons add the "Book of Mormon" and other books to the Bible, while Jehovah Witnesses take away from the Bible by not holding to everything the Bible teaches. Islam holds the Koran as more important than the Bible. Hinduism has the Vedas and on it goes.

John concludes by saying, "Even so, come, Lord Jesus." As we see Bible prophecies being fulfilled before our eyes on almost a daily basis that should be our desire as well, "Even so, come, Lord Jesus!"

If you are already a believer in Jesus then I would challenge you to be living your life as if Jesus could come at any moment.

If you are not a believer in Jesus, I would challenge you to put your faith in him so that you will be saved from this coming 7-year tribulation and ultimately from hell itself.

Jesus was sacrificed on the cross for your sin. He gave his blood in payment for your sin, but you must take that step of faith and call on him for salvation. Jesus died for all, but only those who receive him as their savior from sin have eternal life.

Simply say, "Jesus I know I am a sinner and deserve to die, but I believe you died in my place and that you arose from the dead on the third day. I now put my faith in you, come into my life and cleanse me from my sin and give me eternal life. Thank you, Jesus, Amen."

If you have now put your faith in Jesus you are now a part of God's family and as a part of His family it is important to learn more about living for Him. Reading the Bible, God's Word each day, praying, and attending a good Bible believing church are 3 things you can do right now to grow in your new faith.

If you have any questions or if I can help in any way feel free to email me at: andyferrier@comcast.net

Shalom,
Andy Ferrier

How to Interpret the Bible

One of the first problems in understanding the prophecies given in the Bible is the fact that two people can read the same prophecy in the Bible and come up with two different interpretations of what is being said. For example, Jewish scholars interpret **Isaiah chapter 53** differently than Christian scholars. Let's look at just a few of the verses in this chapter of Isaiah.

Isaiah 53:3-10,

Many Jewish scholars say these verses are talking about the nation of Israel. Christian scholars on the other hand, say these verses are talking about the suffering of Jesus. Both of these interpretations cannot be correct. The way to determine which is correct is to understand how to properly interpret the Bible.

Using a few simple rules to interpret the Bible correctly opens the prophetic passages and the seemingly difficult text. Yes, there are some very difficult passages in the Bible, but for the most part, the Bible is understandable. Here are three simple rules:

Rule #1

Interpret the Bible literally, unless it is clear that a literal interpretation is not intended. For example, when the Bible says that God parted the waters of the Red Sea and the children of Israel walked through on dry land, this should be taken literally. When it says, the Egyptian army was drowned when God made the waters return, there is nothing in the text that would indicate this should not be taken literally. It really happened. It is not a fairy tale or an allegory. Explorers have recently found the remains of Pharaoh's chariots on the bottom of the Red Sea, confirming this miracle. A literal interpretation is taking the text at face value. Another example, this time from the area of prophecy, can be found in:
Zechariah 9:9.

This prophecy was fulfilled literally when Jesus rode into Jerusalem on the back of a donkey (**Matthew 21:1-9**).

For one final example, let's look at a prophecy fulfilled after thousands of years.

In **Amos 9: 14, 15** God spoke of the return of the Jewish people back to their homeland. In 1948, Israel became a nation for the first time in almost 2,000 years. Each year more and more Jewish people are returning back to their ancient homeland. This is what Amos and other Jewish prophets said would happen. It is exciting to see it happening before our very eyes. In fact, I had the wonderful experience of living in Israel for 3 years during the mid 80's. I witnessed thousands of Jewish people returning back to their land just as the prophets said would happen.

Many other examples could be given, but the method of literal interpretation of Scripture will be of value as we work our way through the prophecies.

(There are many times throughout Scripture when figures of speech are used and a literal interpretation is not intended. For example: Rev. 1:4 *"His eyes were as a flame of fire."* Or, in Luke 13:32, Jesus said of Herod, *"Tell that fox."* In John 10:7 Jesus said, *"I am the door."* The text is not saying that eyes are on fire, a man is a fox or that Jesus is a door.)

Rule #2

Interpret the Bible in context. My first year of Bible College I attended Word of Life Bible Institute in upstate New York. One of the first things our professors drilled into our heads was to interpret the Bible in context. Many cults have been started by people taking one verse of Scripture and ripping it out of its context and making it say something it really doesn't say.

Taking a Scripture verse in context means that the verses before and after the verse being considered should also be considered. To give you an example of taking something out of context, look at **Zechariah 13:6** in the King James Version.

Some have taken this verse to be talking about Jesus because of the phrase, "wounds in thine (your) hands." However, if we look at the context of this verse, it will be clear that this verse is not talking about Jesus. **Zechariah 13:2** indicates this is a passage about false prophets.

Verse three explains how he got the wounds.

When the context of this passage is included, it becomes clear that this is not talking about Jesus. This verse is talking about false prophets. It is extremely important to look at the whole context of a passage when interpreting the Bible.

Rule #3

Look-up the exact meaning of key words in the passage you are studying. The Old Testament was written in Hebrew with the exception of a few chapters of Aramaic in the Book of Daniel. The New Testament was written in Greek. Most Bible translations into English are excellent. They were done by highly intelligent and devoted men of God. The translation conveys 99% of the original meaning of the Bible, yet there is always something lost in a translation from one language to another. No translation is perfect. The original language gives a better understanding of the text when the finer points of prophecy are being considered. You do not have to be a Greek or Hebrew scholar to understand Bible prophecy. From time to time I will give you some key words in Greek or Hebrew that will help you to better understand a passage. Word study books, such as a complete concordance, can also be purchased.

Covenant Theology Confusion

In **Romans 11:1** the Apostle Paul asks the question, "Is God finished with Israel? I say then, God has not rejected His people, has He? May it never be! For I too am an Israelite, a descendant of Abraham, of the tribe of Benjamin." His emphatic answer is "May it never be."

Today there are many Christians who would say, "Yes, God is finished with Israel." This view is known as "Replacement" or "Covenant Theology." Part of the teaching of Covenant Theology is that the Church has replaced Israel and is the "New Israel." It is opposed to Dispensational Theology that says Israel and the Church are two separate beings and while God has a plan and program for the Church, He also has a future plan and program for Israel. While Covenant Theology and Dispensational Theology would agree on most areas of doctrine, the one area where there is sharp disagreement has to do with Israel and the Church. Let's look at some of the Scriptures used by Covenant theology.

Romans 2:28, 29 People who hold to Covenant Theology look at this verse and say, "See, it says right here that the real Jews are not the physical Jews but rather spiritual believers in Jesus—the Church."

It is always important when reading the Bible to ask, to whom is the writer talking? In this passage it is clear the Apostle Paul is talking to the Jewish people. Note **Romans 2:17**, "But if you bear the name 'Jew' and rely upon the Law and boast in God."

What he is saying to his own people, the Jewish people, is that it is not enough to be a physical Jew in order to get to Heaven. A Jewish person must become spiritually Jewish as well to gain entrance into Heaven. Many Jewish people in Paul's day and even today believe that just the fact that they are born into a Jewish home guarantees them a spot in Heaven.

Years ago I was playing basketball with a Jewish friend who happened to be an insurance salesman. He was trying to sell me life insurance, and I was trying to sell him "eternal life insurance" through faith in

Jesus as the Messiah!

One day, as we were playing b-ball I asked my friend, "When you die do you know for sure you will go to Heaven?" "Yes, I know for sure I will go to Heaven" was his reply.

"How do you know?" I asked him. "I was very fortunate to be born into a Jewish family and that guarantees me a place in Heaven" was my friends answer.

"So you mean to tell me you can come out here and curse and swear up and down this basketball court, and break God's ten commandments and just because you're Jewish you're going to heaven?" I asked.

"Yes, that's right" my friend said.

Here in Romans two the Apostle Paul says it is not enough to be born into a Jewish family. A Jewish person must become a spiritual Jew, and that only comes through faith in Jesus as the Messiah.

What Paul is NOT saying is that when a gentile (non-Jew) becomes a believer in Jesus he becomes a spiritual Jew. No, he becomes a spiritual gentile. If you were to look up the words "Jew" "Jewish" and "Israel" in the New Testament you will find those words are used over 100 times. But not one time does the New Testament ever say the church has become Israel.

In **1 Corinthians 10:32** Paul says, "Give no offense either to Jews or to Greeks or to the church of God." Paul is saying there are three groups of people in the world today, Jews, Greeks (or gentiles, non-Jews) and the Church. He makes a distinction between the Church and Israel, which is the opposite of what Covenant Theology teaches. Another passage used by Covenant Theology in order to say the Church has replaced Israel is **Romans 9:6-8.**

Covenant Theology interprets this as if Paul is saying the physical Jews are not the real Israel. It is the spiritual Jews who are the real Israel, and that is the church. By examining the context it is clear that Paul is making a distinction here, not between Israel and the Church, but between believing Israel and non-believing Israel. Believing Israel is referred to as "the remnant." In the Old Testament in the days of Elijah, the prophet, there was a remnant of only 7,000 of the millions in Israel who had not bowed down to worship Baal. They were the spiritual Jews. (**1 Kings 19:18**) Today there are a couple hundred thousand Jewish believers in Jesus. They are the remnant Paul is talking about. They are the "children of promise" in this passage. Another passage used by Covenant Theology to teach that the Church is spiritual Israel is **Galatians 3:6, 7.** Paul says that all who believe in Jesus become "sons of Abraham." Doesn't that mean we are spiritual Jews since the Jews are descendants of Abraham? No, and here's why. How many children did Abraham have? Most people immediately answer— two. But after Abraham's first wife, Sarah, died, he remarried and had six more sons. **(Genesis 25:1-4)** If you were a "son of Abraham" your chances of being "Jewish" were only one in eight. To be Jewish you have to be not only from Abraham, but also from Isaac, and Jacob. There are millions of Arabs in the Middle East who claim to be "sons of Abraham" but they are not Jewish. In fact many of them hate the Jews and want to drive Israel into the Mediterranean.

While it is true that all who believe in Jesus are "sons of Abraham," this does not mean all believers in Jesus are spiritual Jews. Jewish believers in Jesus are spiritual Jews, gentile believers are spiritual gentiles. Both are "sons of Abraham."

One other Scripture Covenant Theology uses is **Galatians 6:12-16.** Paul is writing to the gentile churches of Galatia. God had required Abraham and his household to be circumcised. **(Genesis 17)** The gentile believers were being pressured by Jews to be circumcised. Paul is teaching that circumcision is not the issue. Being "a new creation" by faith in Christ is what matters. He adds: "Those who will walk by this rule," (the believers) "peace and mercy be upon them." (these gentile believers) "And upon the Israel of God" would be Jewish believers in Jesus. Covenant

Theology says the "Israel of God" is the Church.

Differences between Israel and the Church:

Church	Israel
Spiritual Seed of Abraham	Physical Seed of Israel
Starts at Pentecost	Starts with Abraham, Isaac and Jacob
Of Many Nations	Of One Nation
Only Believers	Believers and Unbelievers
Spirit Indwells	Spirit Came Upon
Priesthood of Believers	One Family of Priests
Receive Jesus	Most rejected Jesus
Persecuted by Israel	Persecuted the Church
Not a Political State	A Political State

Some Dangers of Covenant Theology

When was the last time you heard a

preacher on T.V. say that God wants you to be healthy, wealthy and prosperous? This is known as the "health, wealth, and prosperity gospel" and it is sweeping our nation today.

How is this teaching justified from Scripture? For the most part the promises God gave to Israel in the Old Testament are applied to the Church today. Since they teach that the Church is the New Israel, and has replaced Israel, the next logical step is to confiscate the promises God gave to Israel. I would hasten to add that many times the curses God gave to Israel are still applied to Israel, but not to the church!

Clearly God did promise Israel health, wealth, and prosperity if they followed and obeyed His laws. **Deuteronomy 28** is one of the longest chapters in the Bible. It describes how God would bless Israel for obedience (and curse Israel for disobedience).

However, the same promises are not given to the Church. Jesus said that in this world we would have tribulation, or lots of problems. (**John 16:33**) The Apostle Paul said he exulted in tribulation. (**Romans 5:3**) Eleven of the twelve apostles were martyred for their faith and in fact lived out their lives in poverty. The Apostle John was not martyred, but he was exiled to the Island of Patmos where he wrote the book of Revelation.

If a group of people should have demonstrated the case for the "health, wealth, and prosperity gospel" it would have been the twelve Apostles, and yet they suffered in poverty. The prosperity gospel continues to be preached and believed because people continue to take the promises God gave to Israel and apply them to the church. This is the practice of Covenant Theology.

Another danger of Covenant Theology is that it can lead to liberalism. By liberalism I mean a denial of the fundamentals of the Christian faith. How does this happen? What fundamentals are denied?

Covenant Theology does not take many of the promises that God gave to Israel as being literal. Many times portions of Scripture are allegorized and spiritualized to make them say things they don't really say. Once this happens, a slippery slope of allegorical interpretation makes it easy for a future generation to deny the faith. If the promises God made to Israel can be explained away, what is next? Can we explain away the death, burial and resurrection of Jesus?

Perhaps the greatest danger of Covenant Theology is that it can and has led to anti-Semitism. Anti-Semitism is a hatred or persecution of the Jewish people solely because they are Jewish. Think about this.

The greatest war our world has seen to date had anti-Semitism as a core principle. Adolf Hitler's hatred of the Jews caused the death of some 60 million people in World War 2.

It is interesting to note that when Hitler rose to power the main teaching of the churches in Germany was that of Covenant or Replacement Theology. Hitler took it to the next level and said if God is finished with the Jews as you say, then let's just get rid of them. Few in the church did anything to stop him. Was it because of their theology? What a person believes does affect the way he lives.

God is not finished with Israel. At this time He is using the Church for His glory and to be His light to a lost and dying world. But there will come a time when He will call the church out of this world. It is called the Rapture of the Church. Then God will once again use the Jewish people to be His witnesses here on earth as is prophesied in chapter seven of the book of Revelation.

Footnotes

The Rapture
1. Renald Showers, Maranatha: Our Lord
Come (Friends of Israel Gospel Gospel
Ministry, Inc. 1995) p.155.
2. ibid., pp. 164-168.
3. Zola Levitt, Levitt Letter Vol. 20 #9.

The Great Deception
5.
http://en.wikipedia.org/wiki/The_War_of_th

e_Worlds_%28radio%29

6. Chuck Missler, Alien Encounters: The Secret behind the UFO Phenomenon (Koinonia House; Revised edition, October 31, 2003).
7. Arnold Fruchtenbaum, The Book of Genesis (Ariel Ministries 2008) p.145-146.
8. http://en.wikipedia.org/wiki/Ra%C3%ABlism
9. Chuck Missler, Alien Encounters: The Secret behind the UFO Phenomenon (Koinonia House; Revised edition, October 31, 2003).
10. John Ankerber, Facts on UFO's (ATRI Publishing January 6, 2010).
11. Chuck Missler, Alien Encounters: The Secret behind the UFO Phenomenon (Koinonia House; Revised edition, October 31, 2003).
12. Ben Stein, Expelled: No Intelligence Allowed Premise Studio, 2008.
13. Chuck Missler, Alien Encounters: The Secret behind the UFO Phenomenon (Koinonia House; Revised edition, October 31, 2003).
14. ibid.
15. ibid.
16. ibid.
17. ibid.

Just before the clock strikes 12!
18.

http://en.wikipedia.org/wiki/David_Koresh
19. http://en.wikipedia.org/wiki/Jim_Jones
20.
http://en.wikipedia.org/wiki/Menachem_Me
ndel_Schneerson
21. Arnold Fruchtenbaum, Footsteps of the
Messiah (Ariel Ministries 2003)
p.634.
22.
http://en.wikipedia.org/wiki/List_of_famines
#20th_century
23. http://en.wikipedia.org/wiki/Spanish_flu
24.
http://en.wikipedia.org/wiki/2004_Indian_O
cean_earthquake
25.
http://en.wikipedia.org/wiki/Dreyfus_affair
26.
http://en.wikipedia.org/wiki/Theodore_Herzl
27.
http://en.wikipedia.org/wiki/Balfour_Declar
ation_of_1917
28. http://en.wikipedia.org/wiki/Palestine
29.
http://www.factsandlogic.org/ad_28.html
30. Stand with us Israel 101 p.40.
31. Arnold Fruchtenbaum The Modern State
of Israel in Bible Prophecy (Ariel
Ministries 2005) p.3
32. ibid. p. 102,103.
33. ibid. p. 207.
34. www.thetempleinstitute.com
35. www.templemountfaithful.org

36. Arnold Fruchtenbaum, Footsteps of the Messiah (Ariel Ministries 2003) p.137-138.

Israel, Islam & Atomic Bombs
37. Seymour Hersh, "The Samson Option" (Random House 1991).
38. Uri Bar-Joseph, "Two Minutes Over Baghdad" (Routledge; 2 edition (May 30, 2003).
39. http://www.usatoday.com/news/world/2005-04-28-israel-bombs_x.htm
40. Arnold Fruchtenbaum, Footsteps of the Messiah (Ariel Ministries 2003) p.107.
41. http://en.wikipedia.org/wiki/Iran
42. http://en.wikipedia.org/wiki/Dead_Sea
43. http://www.adherents.com/largecom/com_at heist.html

9029470R0

Made in the USA
Charleston, SC
04 August 2011